The
Ask Leo!
Guide to
Online Privacy

Protecting yourself from an ever-intrusive world

1st Edition

by

Leo A. Notenboom

An *Ask Leo!*® book
https://askleo.com

ISBN: 978-1-937018-43-6 (PDF)
ISBN: 978-1-937018-44-3 (ebook)
ISBN: 978-1-937018-45-0 (paperback)

CONTENTS

The Ask Leo! Manifesto

I believe personal technology is essential to humanity's future.

It has amazing potential to empower individuals,
but it can also frustrate and intimidate.

I want to make technology work for you.

I want to replace that *frustration* and *intimidation*
with the *amazement* and *wonder* that I feel every day.

I want it to be a *resource* rather than a *roadblock*;
a source of *confidence* rather than *fear*;
a *valuable tool,* instead of a source of *irritation*.

I want personal technology to empower you,
so you can be a part of that amazing future.

That's why *Ask Leo!* exists.

Leo A. Notenboom
https://askleo.com

First: A Freebie for You

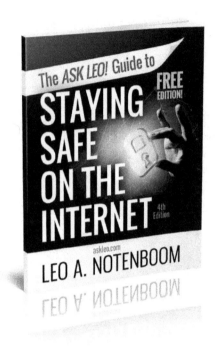

Before we dive in, I have something for you: a copy of ***The Ask Leo! Guide to Staying Safe on the Internet—FREE Edition***. This ebook will help you identify the most important steps you can take to keep your computer, and yourself, safe as you navigate today's digital landscape.

It's yours free when you subscribe to my weekly *Ask Leo!* newsletter.

Each week, you'll find fixes to common problems, tips to keep your computer and online information safe and secure, commentary on technology issues of the day, and even the occasional explanation as to just why things are the way they are. It's educational and fun, and can help you be more effective, more confident, and less frustrated as you use technology.

And it's completely FREE.

Visit https://go.askleo.com/privnews to learn more, browse the archives, and sign up today!

Be Sure to Register Your Book!

Your purchase of this book entitles you to several additional free bonuses.

- All available digital formats of the book as direct downloads. Regardless of which version you purchase, you can enjoy this book on the digital device of your choice.
- Digital updates for life.
- Errata and prioritized Q&A.

You'll find the information you need to register in a chapter near the end of the book. Once you register, you'll be taken to a web page that lists all available bonuses.

INTRODUCTION

Privacy? What Privacy?

Privacy is a *huge* topic. So huge I can't really tell you exactly what steps to take, what settings to change, what apps to avoid, or what services to choose.

Not only are there infinite options, but the options keep changing. In fact, one of the challenges in assembling this book is that I kept coming up with things to ad or update that kept me from pulling the trigger and actually publishing it! (Be sure to subscribe to my newsletter[1] to stay on top of the latest news, updates and information.)

On top of that, there are about as many opinions on the topic as there are internet users. That makes anything I say just one more voice in the crowd …

… not that that's going to stop me. ☺

Two kinds of privacy

"Privacy" is a really big term, and covers many different facets. I want to start by putting a little structure around it. We can lump the various topics two buckets.

Implicit privacy. This is the privacy we assume when we use various online services, modern operating systems, applications, and programs to manage our personal information, data, and activities. Each of them has a set of rules, often codified in some kind of formal privacy policy, that controls exactly what level of access they have to your information, and what they might do with that information as a side effect of your use of their software or service.

Explicit privacy. This is the privacy we control more directly as a result of the choices we make. For example, choosing to share (or not share) a photo on a social media service is one form of explicit privacy, as are the settings we use to control who is allowed to see what we post.

The biggest difference between implicit and explicit privacy, in my mind, is the amount of control we have over it. We implicitly trust that the software and services will do as they say. We explicitly decide what to share based on what we believe may happen.

---

[1] https://newsletter.askleo.com

Privacy, policies, and Big Brother

The privacy—or lack thereof—
assumed when using popular services
or software is always a big topic of
discussion. For example, Windows
10's activity and tracking generated a
great deal of concern as the operating
system became more widely used.
Whether that concern is warranted is
a topic open to debate.

Similarly, using any online service
involves some amount of tracking.
Visiting a simple web site—even *Ask
Leo!*—can result in some amount of
what might be considered "tracking", typically in relation to advertising
displayed on the site. Some people consider that tracking an invasion of privacy.
The most common visible signs are advertisements that appear to follow you
from site to site as you navigate the web.

In reality, all the online services and websites you visit have the ability to collect
vast amounts of data derived from internet users. Similarly, any and all software
you install has the ability to collect usage information.

Whether or not you believe Big Brother is watching, the bottom line is that the
technology is there should he want to.

The (poor) choices we make

At the other end of the privacy spectrum are the often poor choices we make
about what information we share and with whom.

I regularly hear from individuals who share a password with a trusted friend or
significant other, only to be surprised when their privacy is violated in some way
because that trust was unwarranted.

We've all heard stories of individuals losing jobs or job opportunities for statements made, or photos or videos posted on social media. Call your boss names on Twitter, for example, and you have no one to blame but yourself when you're shown the door the next morning. Have you posted "funny" pictures of yourself after imbibing a tad too much alcohol? That could easily be the reason you're not hired for the next job you apply for, or don't get the loan you applied for.

It's sadly common that when it comes to privacy, we're often our own worst enemy.

You're just not that interesting

I've said it over and over: you and I just aren't that interesting as individuals. That your operating system might track what you do is pretty meaningless in terms of personal privacy. That advertisers might use your browser history and things you click on to tailor what you see is similarly pretty benign.

The companies that collect this data aren't looking at you as an individual. They're looking for trends, accumulated data on thousands (if not millions) of users to determine what's being acted on, what's influencing people, and what they might do better.

Even I do it. For example, do I care that you, specifically, looked at my newsletter? At some personal level I do, but I'm not going to sift through information on nearly 60,000 subscribers to see who did and who didn't. On the other hand, if the aggregate number of people who open my newsletter changes in some dramatic way, that's a sign I want to see; that's information I want to act on. I can only do that by tracking the behavior of 60,000 individuals.

The same is true for most any company. Your privacy isn't being violated, because nobody is looking at you, specifically. You're just not that interesting.

But you might be interesting to someone, someday

There are two cases in which you might become "interesting".

If you run afoul of the law. This is a non-issue for most people. But what if you live in an oppressive regime, or are subject to investigation for your activities by whatever law enforcement agencies apply to your situation? Even this falls into two sub-categories: the unduly paranoid (sadly, a larger number than one might hope), and the legitimately concerned, for both legal and illegal reasons.

It is important to realize that if you fall into this category (again, depending on where you live), law enforcement may have the right to collect information about you. This can include information we normally brush off as irrelevant, like ad or service usage information collected by your ISP, or the services and software you use. I have to say law enforcement *may* have the right, because laws differ dramatically depending on where you live. Of more practical import, perhaps, law enforcement capabilities also often vary dramatically based on everything from expertise to budget to prioritization of where they choose to expend their limited resources.

Future opportunities. The other case is the one I alluded to earlier: some years from now, perhaps someone will research your history as part of a job application, or something else where your record and your reputation are important. What you post publicly (and in some cases, even privately) today may influence their opinion tomorrow.

It's all so scary. What to do?

It'd be easy to read that last section, throw up your hands, and crawl into a hole thinking privacy is a thing of the past, at least when it comes to the internet.

Certainly, if you're a criminal, you should be concerned. The only thing really preventing you from being exposed is the limited resources of the various and sundry law enforcement agencies who really do care about you, specifically. There are steps you should take, but I'm not the one to help you take them.

For the rest of us living more mundane lives, my advice is pretty simple.

First: *stop worrying about being tracked* by the companies that provide the services you use. As I said, they don't care about you as an individual. Certainly there is much room for policy debate about what kinds of information they should and should not collect, and how they should or should not use it, but in my opinion, this has little chance of impacting you as an individual. (And if you're going to worry, then be more consistent. It's always funny to me to get rants about the alleged privacy violations of company "A", sent via an email address provided by company "B", whose activity is on par with "A". Honestly, if the behaviors of the major service providers really concern you that much, I know of no solution other than to walk away from the internet entirely.)

Second*: don't post anything you don't want made public.* Learn the privacy policies and settings of your social media and other applications, and change them and/or change your behavior accordingly. Public once is public forever; there's no calling it back. Think twice about what you post privately as well, since you're assuming your private audience won't someday make it public without your approval. This includes social media, but also things you share in any form, be it email, text messaging, or other media. We've all seen situations where communications once thought private were made public, to great embarrassment or worse.

Privacy remains your responsibility

I remain a strong believer in our wonderfully interconnected world and all the opportunities it presents.

Naturally, it brings risk as well as reward.

Ultimately, it's our responsibility to be aware of those risks, educate ourselves about the possibilities as well as the practical realities, and make careful choices accordingly.

Giving Away Our Privacy

I often remind folks on my Facebook Fan Page[2] not to post personal information. (I delete posts that contain that kind of stuff, as I do in comments on *Ask Leo!* articles.) It got me to thinking a little.

On one hand, we rail against the supposed loss of privacy posed by the various services we use and companies behind them, not to mention concerns that various governments might be doing some kind of snooping.

And yet, we give away our private information—even posting it publicly— without hesitation.

Lack of understanding?

Part of it, I suppose, could be a lack of understanding.

Perhaps people don't understand that when they post something on a Facebook fan page, anyone can see it. Perhaps they think it's a direct and private line to me, somehow, in spite of the fact that they can see everyone else's postings to me alongside their own.

Perhaps folks don't understand that comments posted on *Ask Leo!* are not only visible to anyone who happens to come by, but are regularly spidered by the search engines and archived by internet archive sites. Not only is what's posted in a comment public, but once posted, it can never be completely removed from the internet, even if it is removed from my site.

And yet, with all the publicity internet privacy has received of late, shouldn't people understand that "public" is now more public than it's ever been? Quite literally billions of people could potentially see what you post.[3]

---

[2] https://facebook.com/askleofan
[3] No, I'm not saying billions *will*; I'm saying that any of the billions of people on the internet today *could*.

Disregard for consequences?

People post email addresses online all the time—and then wonder why they get spam.

Try this: go to twitter.com (you won't need an account) and search for hotmail.com. Or gmail.com. Have a look at how many people have committed their email address—often their personal, private email address—to the permanently public Twitter archive. I understand that businesses do so as part of their publicity, but I see too many individuals posting their private personal email addresses without realizing what they're in for.

In the old days, Usenet was the place for spammers to harvest email address. I'm sure Twitter is a veritable gold mine for them.

And phone numbers? Would you put your phone number on a bathroom wall for anyone to see? Of course not. So why are people posting them on blog comments and Facebook pages? They're opening themselves up to all sorts of potential abuse or harassment.

Privacy is your responsibility too

Yes, we should absolutely be ever watchful for corporate and government abuses of individual privacy.

But privacy starts at home. Much as with malware prevention, individuals are often the weakest link in the chain.

Watch who you're giving your information to—and this goes well beyond email addresses and phone numbers. Just because a form randomly pops up asking for something doesn't mean you have to give it (or that it has to be accurate). Use common sense and good judgment.

And as with so many things on line, be skeptical.

Vulnerable Points on the Path to Privacy

Privacy and security are more important, and under greater threat, than ever before. We manage an ever-increasing amount of sensitive information and tasks, while the number of ways our information can be exposed seems to be exploding.

There are five major areas in which your security and privacy can be both exposed and protected:

1. Your computer, including all the software on it, and the hardware itself.
2. Your network, the vital link that connects your computers to each other and to the internet, is a potential point of major exposure.
3. Your ISP, the provider of that vital link, wields more power and is subject to more scrutiny than most realize.
4. Your online services: they hold your data, but do they know what they're doing, and will they defend your privacy if needed?
5. You, your friends, and acquaintances: often the weakest link in the chain. Do the people you interact with value (or understand) privacy and security as much as you do? Do you yourself practice thoughtful security measures?

Let's review each of these points of risk, exposing the technological hazards we (perhaps unknowingly) face every day.

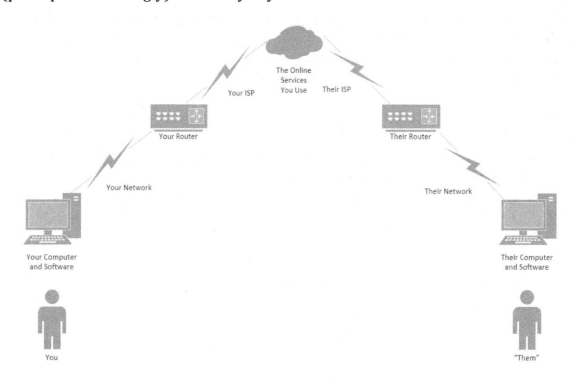

1. Your Computer

Privacy and security start at home (or, in the case of cell phones, in your pocket).

Software

For every piece of software we run, we trust that the right decisions have been made in terms of maintaining our privacy and security. We also trust the vendors themselves have our best interests in mind. This is true not only for our desktop and mobile computers and phones, but for the surprising number of network-connected devices in our lives, including televisions, cars, security cameras, and even baby monitors.

The operating system

Be it Windows, Linux, Mac OS, or something else, most of our technology runs some form of base operating system software, or "OS". Even those devices we consider to be single purpose, like a baby monitor, often run a "general purpose" operating system (typically, a Linux variant).

When Windows 10 changed its approach to privacy, it became shockingly clear how much we rely on Windows for privacy and security. Many felt Microsoft had crossed a line, collecting excessive amounts of information in ways outside our control. Exactly what was being shared was unclear, and there were no trustworthy, easy-to-use solutions to avoid it. While Microsoft appears to have added more privacy controls to subsequent versions, the fact remains that for many, trust was irrevocably breached.

The most important take-away, however, is not that Microsoft may or may not be trustworthy; it's that every operating-system vendor has the power do any or all of this, with or without letting us know. The amount of trust we place in any OS vendor to properly manage our privacy and security is *enormous*.

Aside from being vigilant, managing the privacy and security options that are available, and paying attention to reliable, objective news sources, there's little we can do if our trust is misplaced, other than switching to a more trustworthy alternative.

Applications

Everything I've just said about operating systems applies to every piece of software running on your computer, phone, or other device—including security software.

The average computer user has dozens, if not hundreds, of apps and applications installed across various devices, from nearly as many different vendors—and each vendor has its own approach to privacy and security.

That's a lot of trust spread across a lot of different companies. Besides trusting that they're competent at whatever it is we use their software for, we're also assuming they're competent at keeping our information safe and secure—and that they aren't, themselves, malicious. We often give them much more access to our information than we realize.

The best defense here is twofold:
- Don't install things you don't need.
- Only install from reputable vendors.

Malware

When people think about privacy and security on their own computers, the first thing they think of is malware: malicious software that somehow makes it onto their computer and proceeds to steal information (or worse).

I've placed it last in the software category, because by now, most people understand malware and the concepts behind it. More importantly, we know how to combat it. It's something that makes the news almost every day. And while protecting yourself from malware is terribly important, it's a topic already well understood.

You know how to combat malware. You know how to avoid malware. You know how to be skeptical. It's something this industry talks about every day, so I won't belabor it here.

Hardware

An often-overlooked aspect of security is what I refer to as "physical security". One of my frequent statements is, "If it's not physically secure, it's not secure." If someone untrustworthy can touch your hardware, they can do amazing amounts of damage.

Physical access

If someone can walk up to your computer (or phone, or router, or many other networked devices) and start using it, that's a privacy and security hole bigger than anything I've listed so far. If someone malicious has access to your device, they can do anything.

Most of the time, our concern is theft. The good news here is that most thieves are unsophisticated. They're just looking to turn the hardware around for some quick cash—they don't really care what you have stored on it. However, that data is certainly accessible to them—or the person they sell it to—should either of them have a little technical expertise.

More commonly, the risks are closer to home: spouses, co-workers, children, and friends. Be they malicious or nosy, the people around us often have the greatest incidental access to our things. It's one thing to go snooping around our medicine cabinet, but something else entirely to poke around in our email, spreadsheets, or other personal data.

How much of a problem this is varies, of course. At one extreme, you may not feel the need to take much action. At the other, a combination of encryption, software locks, and perhaps even hardware locks might be appropriate.

Hardware compromise

We usually trust that the hardware we use hasn't been compromised. That may not be a safe assumption when using devices in public.

A good example is a hardware key-logger inserted between the computer and keyboard. Undetectable to any software on the machine, and hidden behind the computer itself, it can passively collect massive amounts of information until the perpetrator comes along to pick it up and act on the data.

While it's significantly less common than other forms of compromise, hardware hacking can take many forms. It's one reason I never use a public computer for anything remotely sensitive.

2. Your Network

Much of the risk we encounter every day is due to being inter-connected, or networked. It's also what enables so many of the features, functionality, and rich experience we enjoy with technology. Your network is how your computers are connected to each other and to the world.

Router

Typically, the first device the internet reaches on entering your home or workplace is a single router. Its job is to allow your multitude of devices to share a single internet connection. As a side effect, it also acts as a security device itself: routers are great firewalls, protecting your network from many of the threats out on the internet.

Routers are powerful devices. In fact, they're powerful *computers*. They're often based on general-purpose operating systems. Before even plugging the device in, we're trusting that the router vendor is competent and has factored in appropriate measures to protect our privacy and security.

Even then, routers are interesting to hackers, because by compromising a router, they can compromise all the devices connected to it, or misdirect people into visiting malicious sites or downloading malware.

Beyond getting a reputable device from a reputable vendor, the single most important solution in your control is to secure your router. Every router comes with default settings that may or may not be the most secure configuration for you.

Wireless connections

Wireless connections are often controlled by your router, but deserve additional attention. They're an easy point of compromise, particularly in public.

Because the range of a wireless connection is a function of both the wireless access point and the computer attempting to connect, it's possible to connect from a distance further than most people might realize. Particularly if someone is dedicated to the effort and trying to connect to a relatively close access point, it's unwise to rely on distance alone as a security measure.

The most important thing you can do in your home and business is to never have an open Wi-Fi hotspot; always use a WPA2 key or password for the connection.

The most important thing you can do when traveling is to know how to use an open Wi-Fi hotspot safely.

Other computers

I mentioned earlier that your router protects you from many of the threats coming from the internet. What if the threat is more local?

Many people fail to realize that their computers and networks are often set up to give locally connected machines—machines on the same side of the router—a high level of trust. Sometimes, that trust is unwarranted.

Consider your child's computer. He or she may not have the sophistication to know not to download and run malware, and a lack of adequate protection could infect other machines connected to the same local network. The same could be true of a visitor, or even a less-than-tech-savvy spouse. Sometimes, the threats come from within.

Solutions involve making sure your computer has its own defenses set properly, including its own firewall. Today these are on by default for most devices. More extreme might be segmenting your network into trusted and untrusted zones, using an additional router or a router that provides this functionality natively.

Other devices

There's been much made of the so-called "internet of things", or IoT. I alluded to this earlier when I discussed devices we would consider dedicated to a single task—such as your refrigerator—that nonetheless run general purpose operating systems.

It turns out neither privacy nor security were at the top of many IoT vendors' feature lists.

The good news is that their negligence has (thus far) mostly been limited to those devices becoming part of botnets used to cause havoc elsewhere. Other than using their owner's internet bandwidth, little damage was done at home. Unfortunately, the potential still exists for more localized damage should hackers ever decide to focus their attentions on it.

The bad news is that, aside from avoiding these devices completely, there's little in our control. Once again, we're limited to using information sources we trust to provide us with reviews and recommendations, now with an eye to privacy and security—an odd concept to consider when looking at an internet-connected television or kitchen appliance.

3. Your ISP

ISP: Internet Service Provider. Depending on where you live (or how you travel), you may have several options, or very few. Regardless of which you choose, you place a tremendous amount of faith in your ISP.

Home internet connection

Connecting to the internet at home has become one of the fundamental utilities folks rely on. Your ISP provides your digital lifeline: your connection to the internet.

Here's the catch: your ISP can monitor your traffic. All of it. Unless you take additional steps, just about anything that travels over your ISP-provided connection can be examined—often in detail—or even recorded by the technicians operating the equipment.

Normally, that's not much of an issue. Your ISP is too busy just keeping the lights on, so to speak, to pay attention to your emails or web browsing. Of greater concern are those situations when your ISP can be compelled to disclose your location and web usage by government demands or court orders.

The average computer user probably doesn't need to be concerned. I know I'm not. But if you are, then the steps you can take generally revolve around encrypting the data that travels between your computer and your ISP.

- https encrypts the connection between websites that support it and your computer. Your ISP can still see that you connected to askleo.com, for example, but they can't see what it is you asked about or looked at.
- A VPN encrypts all traffic between your computer and the VPN service. Your ISP only sees that you've connected to the VPN, but can see nothing beyond that.
- TOR—The Onion Router—is a web proxy (most securely used with a dedicated TOR browser) that encrypts all your web activity, and routes your traffic in such a way that the server to which you are connecting has no idea who you are, unless you explicitly tell them. Once again, your ISP can see that you're using TOR; they just can't see what you're using it for.

One of the most overlooked aspects of this topic is the very literal nature of the term "ISP". Anyone who provides you with a connection to the internet is your ISP. Be it at home, in a hotel, at a coffee shop, or at work (which I'll discuss next), anyone who provides you with an internet connection can examine what you're up to.

Work internet connection

When you're at work, a separate set of rules often apply. Thus, there are several other aspects related to your privacy and security to consider.

- If you're using employer-provided equipment, everything I said about hardware compromise could be at play. It's possible, and possibly quite legal[4], for an employer to install either hardware, software, or both, to monitor your activities at any level of detail they wish.

- If you're using employer-provided internet, then in addition to being your ISP, with all the power that entails, they may be legally allowed to monitor your traffic, even to the point of using techniques to intercept encrypted https traffic.
- When at your place of employment, your private equipment may or may not be subject to your employer's rules and abilities.
- Regardless of whether or not the company cares to monitor what you do, or even compromise your security, you'll still be required to abide by the company's rules.

The best advice I can give here is to have a clear understanding of your workplace's rules and capabilities, and follow them to the letter. Then, depending on your level of trust, take care to isolate anything personal from their network, equipment, and possibly even facilities.

Coffee shops and public locations

Open Wi-Fi at coffee houses is rife with well-known security and privacy issues. You likely already know how to stay safe using open Wi-Fi.

It's important to realize that those steps may not protect you from the owner of the coffee shop or Wi-Fi provider. When using their internet, *they are your ISP*, and as such may have access to all the abilities I mentioned above.

To avoid the issues surrounding wireless connections, many people choose to use a wired connection instead. Unfortunately, the provider of that connection still has all the capabilities of an ISP, and could compromise your privacy and security. In the worst case, they could also be slightly incompetent, and expose your connection to other network users, making it just as vulnerable as open Wi-Fi.

Remember to treat any internet connection from an unknown or untrusted source with skepticism.

---

[4] Caveat: I'm no lawyer, and this is in no way legal advice. Since laws vary dramatically around the world, consult an appropriate attorney for advice relating to your specific situation and location.

Shared connections

One scenario I often hear is what I'll simply call a "shared" connection. Sharing can take just about any form the name implies:

- Using (with or without permission) the internet connection belonging to a neighbor.
- Using the internet connection belonging to your host when visiting friends or family.
- Using the internet connection provided by a landlord.
- Etc.

Unfortunately, many people don't realize that each one of these situations, and many others like them, place the owner of the internet connection in the role of internet provider. In other words, they're the ISP, and once again have all the capabilities associated with that.

Keep this in mind: when visiting a friend, your ISP is not their ISP; your ISP is your friend.

4. Your Online Services

When we talk about privacy, many people immediately think of online services. Given the regular news reports we hear of breaches at major providers, it's important to keep the online services we use in mind.

But the topic is both deeper and wider than that. We often fail to consider all of the online services we use. On top of that, we fail to recognize that these services are themselves subject to various laws and regulations that can further put our privacy and security at risk.

Email

Email is a lifeline almost everyone online relies on[5]. It's been around for decades, and represents what might be considered the first cloud service, before "the cloud" was even a thing. We regularly share our lives, our stories, and of late, our private information with friends, family, businesses, and more, all via email.

---

[5] Or will when they enter the workforce. ☺

For the most part, email is all unencrypted. <u>Our email provider can read it all</u>. In fact, anyone with access to the servers between our email interface and our message's destination can access it as it passes through.

The good news is that there is so much email that, once again, we'd need to be pretty interesting for anyone to bother paying attention to what we have to say. Chances are, we're not.

I'd love to be able to provide a simple, easy solution, but I don't have one. Encryption is key, but email encryption is a mess. <u>There are techniques</u>, but they're often cumbersome and not universally compatible.

Most important to your privacy and security is to be aware of the limitations of "plain old email".

Social Media

Overshare much? When it comes to social media—meaning services like Facebook, Twitter, Instagram, and others—we are often our own worst enemies. Not understanding the ramifications of such visibility, people often share more than they should. This isn't just about pictures of the drunken party that come back to bite someone when they apply a job; it runs from unexpected embarrassment to online harassment.

Social media providers have a wide variety of terms and conditions that allow them to do pretty much whatever they want with the information you post. Most aren't interested in doing anything, but be it accidental or under legal pressure, providers have been known to take action that unexpectedly exposed more than the user intended.

The key things to remember when it comes to social media are:
- You're probably sharing more than you think.
- You're almost definitely sharing to more people than you think.
- The provider can be compelled to provide your access logs and what you post to the authorities.
- There is no "undo". Once you post something, it's stored somewhere, for much longer than you think.

Share wisely.

Storage

Cloud storage is awesome. It really is. As backing up is one of the themes I beat to death regularly, the number of additional options online storage created is wonderful. There's little excuse these days to lose more than a few minutes of work, even in the worst of disasters.

With that convenience comes privacy and security issues.

The single biggest issue with cloud storage is that the provider of the storage service has access to your data. When you think about it, *they must have access* to provide the service. That, then, exposes two risks:

- The service provider (or its employees) can peek at your stuff.
- The service provider can be compelled to provide your stuff to the authorities.

One of the themes you might recognize here is the solution: encryption. For example, using a utility like BoxCryptor to transparently encrypt the files you store online ensures those files are accessible only to you.

Connectivity services

One of the solutions for many types of network risk is the use of a VPN, or Virtual Private Network. This is often a fine and appropriate solution. It ensures that your entire internet conversation, from your computer to the VPN service itself, is encrypted and hidden from prying eyes. It's a solution often recommended for people who travel a lot and might need to make use of questionable internet services.

What most don't realize, however, is that using a VPN simply replaces one set of risks with another.

In a very real sense, the VPN service becomes your ISP. They provide a private, encrypted connection between you and their service. From that point, your connection continues onto the public internet.

The VPN has provided your connection to the internet, and like any ISP, that implies *they* can see what you're up to.

Many people focus on speed when choosing a VPN provider. VPNs add additional processing and latency to your online communications, and can slow it down— sometimes significantly—depending on the provider.

More important, I would assert, is choosing a VPN service you can trust. Not only do you need to trust their implementation of VPN technology, but also that they're not accessing, or otherwise allowing others to access, your data. Realize, too, many VPNs are based in other countries, or have a presence in other countries, which means they may be subject to the laws of countries other than your own.

Professional services

The banking industry frustrates me. In fact, I'll just say that I find the whole financial sector frustrating at times. While there are some good players out there who really understand privacy and security and manage it well, there are many who aren't quite as on top of things as they should be. From sending out legitimate mail that looks like spam to outdated password requirements that are fundamentally unsecure, much of the industry is still playing "catch up" compared to many others.

It's no real coincidence that many of the major hacks we hear about are in financial services.

Fortunately, your money is generally protected in the banking world. With other professional services, such as online bookkeeping, bill paying, financial reporting, and more, things are more haphazard.

When choosing an online professional service, or whether to use one provided by your bank or someone else, I'd recommend looking for a few things:
- The ability to use arbitrary-length passwords, including spaces.
- The availability of two-factor authentication.
- Telephone support that gets you to real people who speak your native language.
- If applicable, the availability of real-time transaction alerts.
- And of course, https, and only https, on every related website and page.

Online services can be used safely. I use them myself regularly. But here more than anywhere else, privacy and security is a partnership between a service that knows what it's doing, and you, making appropriate security-related choices.

Account management

Once again, you may be your own worst enemy.

In my experience, most incidents of account hacking, theft, and loss are *completely preventable*. I see people making mistakes every day that eventually lead to account compromise. The service involved isn't at fault, and the hackers are simply taking advantage of those mistakes.

Ultimately, privacy, and most assuredly security, is *your* responsibility. You may feel like it's someone else's—the service, the software, or the coffee shop—but ultimately, **you** choose which services, software, and coffee shops to use, and you choose whether or not to use them in a secure manner.

Sometimes I wonder if people *want* to get hacked, because I see them neglecting the basics of safe account management:
- Choose appropriate passwords.
- Manage passwords appropriately to keep them private.
- Set up account recovery, especially two-factor authentication, and don't let such options expire.

5. Your friends and acquaintances

One of the odder (yet relatively common) questions I get is whether video chat can be intercepted and recorded. The short answer is, as long as you're using a reputable service, it's highly unlikely.

But there's a bigger risk that most folks seem to overlook: the person at the other end. *They* can record it. It's a common method of extortion: someone is lured into a salacious online chat, which is recorded by the person at the other end, who threatens to release the video unless payment is made.

This highlights one of the greatest risks we face: the person at the other end.

I'm not saying they have malicious intent. But when you communicate with someone, your information is flowing across their network and devices as well as your own.

Ultimately, we're assuming this other person is not being spied on, and knows how to keep his or her system and environment secure.

In addition, we're trusting they don't actually have malicious intent. Everything we send, every picture we share—even with a limited audience—they can in turn share with whomever they please, including the entire world.

Your responsibility

At first glance, privacy and security issues may seem overwhelming and disheartening. It's easy to feel beleaguered, and even annoyed, that the digital world isn't a safer place.

Personally, I feel the privilege of playing and working on the internet, and the multitude of opportunities it presents, makes it worth staying on top of what I need to do to use it safely.

That includes learning who to trust, and taking the steps I need to take to keep my identity, reputation, data, and devices protected.

What Does It Mean for a Source to Be "Reputable"?

One of the very common recommendations folks in my position make is that you only purchase or download software from reputable sources.

Naturally, we also get the follow-up question: how do you know whether or not a source has a good reputation and is "reputable"?

While there are no hard-and-fast rules, I can offer some guidelines on who to trust.

Prior experience

It's human nature to trust those with whom we've had good experiences. In fact, that's how reputations are built: one customer at a time. The more happy customers a service has, the better their overall reputation, and the more "reputable" they are. If you're one of those happy customers, it's quite natural and appropriate to trust them with your next purchase. If you've had personal experience with a source and been happy with the results, that's perhaps the single biggest *personal* indicator that your trust might be warranted.

As I said, though, it does assume you've already had some experience. If you're starting from scratch, you need to look elsewhere for information.

Trusted recommendations

Chances are you have other sources you already trust.

Your friends and acquaintances, for example, may have relevant experience. Based on your comfort with their expertise, savvy, and opinions in general, they can be reasonable sources of information. They may be able to tell you resources they like and trust, or they can offer their opinion about a source you're considering.

Similarly, online information sites that you already trust—perhaps *Ask Leo!,* for example—are also good sources to consult. Often these sites have explicit recommendations and opinions of their own, in addition to commentary left by site visitors. Naturally, blind trust is never warranted, but as an additional source of data, websites can be useful in determining a source's overall reputation.

Reputable name brands

While it's a weaker sense of reputation, one of the common pieces of advice I give is to stick to "name brands". In other words, a company you've heard of is probably more reputable than one you haven't.

Indeed, some "name brands" have very strong reputations. Knowing they've been around for many years tells you they're not some fly-by-night operation that'll disappear as soon as you have a problem.

Conversely, if you've never heard of the source, choosing to trust them is a little riskier. It's not a reason to avoid them completely—all brands have to start somewhere—but it does mean you'll want to approach them with a more skeptical eye.

Online reputation

One of the most common approaches to determining whether a company, service, product, or even individual is worthy of trust is to fire up your favorite search engine and see what "the internet" has to say. For example, searching for "<company>", where "<company>" is the name of the source or service you're evaluating, is a start. Refining the search to look for specific topics, like "<company> support", "<company> horror", or even "<company> sucks" can lead to interesting information.

One of the things I like to do when evaluating a software vendor is to visit their support forums. I look for a few specific things:

- What are people complaining about? (Support forums are where you bring problems and complaints, after all, so don't be too concerned if complaints are all you find.)
- Are there company representatives present, or does the forum offer only peer support?
- Are problems addressed by the company?
- How quickly does the company respond to issues?
- What is the overall "feel" of the community? Has the vendor made the majority of customers angry, or is there a sense that many people walk away happy?

Not every product or service has a support forum to look into, but when they do, it's a valuable resource for product evaluation. I've even suspended recommendations based on what I've found in support forums.

Another source for valuable information is to check ratings on sites like Amazon, if the product is listed there. You don't have to buy from Amazon[6], but browsing the feedback and Q&A left by others can be enlightening.

Perfection doesn't exist

Perhaps the single hardest aspect of evaluating reputation information, be it from trusted friends or random internet searches, is the wide variety of opinions you find. For any given company, service, or product, you'll find people who absolutely love it, people who absolutely hate it, and all flavors in-between.

Two things to remember when evaluating reputation online:
- People go online to complain. Those who have good experiences rarely post about it. That can lead to a false sense of negativity surrounding whatever it is you're looking into.
- Every product or service has flaws or bugs. While the number and severity of those issues is important, how they're handled is even more so. Be it product and service updates, or just good customer service, how a company deals with issues is perhaps the single most important characteristic of what it means to be "reputable".

---

[6] Though, for a variety of reasons, I almost always do. They have, in my opinion, a very good reputation as a seller, reseller, and a source of good information.

When you find complaints, see if the issue is real or not, consider whether the issue would even apply to your situation, and see if and how the company handles it. There will always be people who will never, ever, be happy—people for whom only perfection will do—so you need to use your own judgment as to how seriously to consider their feedback.

Price isn't everything

Please don't make price your only criteria.

Price is a very important factor in many purchasing decisions, but realize that "you get what you pay for" is more true than most people realize. Lower cost often comes at the expense of after-sale service, or, even worse, at the expense of including a few PUPs, or occasionally malware, with your downloads.

Be price conscious, of course, but consider it one of many factors that go into deciding whether or not to make a purchase and ultimately trust a software or service vendor.

When in doubt, ask

One of the best tools you have at hand is a set of trusted resources you can ask when you're not sure.

Friends, acquaintances, online communities, user groups, technical support sites—all of these can be places to ask your questions prior to deciding where to place your trust.

"Reputable" is all about "reputation", and asking around is one of the best ways to find out exactly what that reputation is.

PRIVACY ISSUES: YOUR COMPUTER'S SOFTWARE

Do you trust your operating system? Do you even have an idea of what all it can do? How about all the programs you have installed on your computer or mobile device—are they trustworthy?

We often worry a great deal about external threats to our privacy—hacks and other kinds of information leaks online—without really considering what's happening right here, at home, on our desk or in our pocket.

The reality can actually be quite frightening once you think about it: the software you use every day has an incredible amount of access. In fact, it's safe to say that it can pretty much access everything and anything that you might use on or via your computer.

As you can imagine, this is worth a little thought.

We'll start at the beginning.

Privacy Begins with the Operating System

With the release of Windows 10, Microsoft took a lot of heat for particularly permissive default privacy settings, as well as being unclear about exactly what information was sent back to Microsoft, and under what conditions.

While they've addressed some of those issues since, it all serves to highlight an important concept that many people all too readily overlook: the operating system on your machine has a tremendous capability to protect or violate your privacy.

Do you trust it?

The OS sees all and knows all

The operating system on your computer is the interface between all of your software and hardware and the rest of the world.

When an application wants to read from the disk, it does so via the operating system. If an application wants to communicate on the network or internet, it uses the operating system. Even when an application just wants to display something to ask you a question, it's the operating system that displays the message and collects your response.

This puts the operating system in a unique position to see absolutely everything you do, because it's instrumental in making anything you do happen at all.

It's something we rarely think about, at least until things like the furor over Windows 10. Then things change, a little or a lot; but in the long run, the issue blows over, because we need to get on with our work. The fundamental power of the operating system, and that it's in such a unique position to examine all we do, fades to the background again.

It's not just Windows

I use the Windows 10 release as an example because it made a lot of news at the time, and because so many people use Microsoft Windows.

But before you start pointing fingers, it's critical to realize that *every* operating system has this level of access to what you're doing. Be it Mac OS, iOS, Linux, Android, or something else completely, by the nature of what they do, all operating systems are in position to examine, record, and report back anything they care to.

It's not that they *do*; it's that they *can*. It's not something malicious or even surprising. A fundamental side effect of giving an OS the power to do its job also gives it the power to examine what's going on.

How do you know it's not sharing that information with others? Well, as an average computer user, you really can't.

It all boils down to trust.

If you don't trust it, why are you using it?

One of the more frustrating aspects of my job is hearing people rail against some large entity like Microsoft, Apple, or Google, all the while using the software and/or services provided by—you guessed it—Microsoft, Apple, or Google.

It might sound a little brutal, but the bottom line is simple: if you really don't trust Microsoft Windows[7], for example, don't use it. That could be as extreme as never, ever using it, or it could be more strategic, choosing to avoid it for certain types of activities you consider particularly sensitive. Either way, "fixing" the operating system is not an option, so the only true options you have are:

- Live with it.
- Avoid it for specific areas of concern.
- Avoid it completely.

---

[7] For any reason, really. If you don't trust their privacy protections, security, or overall capability, then avoiding their product would be the thing to do. Even if that's all OK to you, perhaps you don't trust that they won't change something out from underneath you in a future version. Either way, it all comes back to trust.

And again, while Microsoft Windows is my example, these statements apply equally to any software vendor whose products you choose to use.

Alternatives to consider

When we talk about alternatives to operating systems, we're really asking the question, "Who do you trust?" As I've said repeatedly, using any operating system means placing some degree of trust in a product.

When it comes to desktop and laptop PCs, this typically means either:
- Windows: you're trusting Microsoft.
- Mac: you're trusting Apple.
- Linux: you're trusting an army of independent developers (as well as the sponsor of the particular distribution you're using).

When it comes to tablets and mobile devices, the choices are:
- Android and Chrome OS: you're trusting Google, and to some degree Linux.
- iOS: you're trusting Apple.

Oh, and in almost all cases, if your device come pre-loaded with the operating system (as many do these days), you're also trusting the vendor of the device, since they can and do add things.

As I said, the question really does boil down to: of those alternatives, whom do you trust?

Or, perhaps, who do you distrust the least?

The pragmatic reality

Operating systems and the privacy implications they bring are truly much too complex for the average consumer to completely understand. We shouldn't *have* to get that deep an understanding, or we'd never have time to actually move on to whatever it is we're trying to accomplish!

In many ways, some privacy exposure is part of the cost of using today's complex systems. For any system you use, information is likely being shared "upstream" for a variety of reasons, ranging from beneficial and benign (such as information used to make the software better) to malicious and invasive (such as truly tracking what you as an individual are doing).[8]

Unfortunately, we might also find ourselves faced with constraints—software we rely on that only runs on an OS we don't trust, or cross-platform compatibility issues with people we work with on a regular basis, for example—that might force us to rely on an OS we'd prefer to avoid.

In situations like this, it's important to understand what's possible, and take whatever steps you feel are appropriate.

As for me, I run almost all the operating systems I've mentioned here (except iOS, for no reason other than time) and honestly have few concerns. I trust that any information these operating systems transmit "home" is either inconsequential, appropriately anonymized, or appropriately protected, and serves to make the software and my experience using it better.

I also know not everyone agrees with my approach.

---

[8] My stance remains: you and I simply aren't interesting enough for this level of detailed, personal tracking. But it's important to understand that the possibility exists.

Are There Hidden Files that Save Every Keystroke I've Ever Typed?

This is a relatively persistent family of questions that comes around from time to time, particularly in times of concern about individual privacy.

There are several misconceptions in the question.

Further, those misconceptions are based on kernels of truth, which means I can't just say "that's wrong"; instead, it's more a case of "it's not like that—it's like this".

Let's see if I can clear up the confusion. To do so, we'll need to talk about keystrokes, loggers, hidden files, erasing files, and *really* erasing files.

Recording keystrokes

There is no hidden file containing every keystroke you've ever typed on your computer.

Pragmatically, if every keystroke were being recorded somehow, there's no way, after all this time, it would still be some kind of secret. We'd be hearing about a lot more successful prosecution of cyber criminals, along with a plethora of lawsuits regarding various privacy concerns.

So, no, there is no hidden permanent record of every keystroke recorded by the operating system, drivers, or other official software.

However, there are kernels of truth:

- As I write this, every keystroke is being recorded to create this article. That's what we would expect. The documents you create, the emails you send, are all a type of record of your keystrokes.
- Every keystroke is temporarily recorded in keyboard buffers. These allow you to "type ahead" while your computer is doing something else. Once the computer's ready again, everything you typed suddenly appears. Those buffers range anywhere from a few bytes to several thousand, and as they fill up, older keystrokes are removed to make room. Normally they're in memory only; turn your computer off, and they're gone. There may also be

one in your actual keyboard, but again, turn the power off, and it's gone too.

- Keyboard buffers may be written to disk-swap files as the operating system manages memory between all the running programs. If you turn off your computer, the swap file remains, and could be recovered and examined for "interesting" contents. It's easy to get the swap file, but extremely difficult to make sense of its contents. There's also no predicting what the swap file will contain, or for how long.

It's also worth remembering that all bets are off if you have malware.

Keystroke loggers

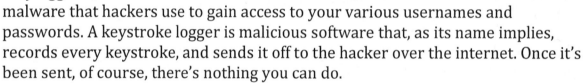

Keystroke loggers, or "keyloggers", are a form of malware that hackers use to gain access to your various usernames and passwords. A keystroke logger is malicious software that, as its name implies, records every keystroke, and sends it off to the hacker over the internet. Once it's been sent, of course, there's nothing you can do.

I often hear from people who wonder if one technique or another will somehow "bypass" keyloggers, allowing them to log in safely without the keylogger logging anything. The answer is no. There are two important points to realize about keyloggers:

- A keylogger is "just" malware that happens to log keystrokes.
- As malware, a keylogger can also do anything else it wants—including logging whatever fancy trick you use to try to bypass it.

From my perspective, malware, including keystroke loggers, is the only practical reason for concern when it comes to keeping any record of your keystrokes.

The good news is that since keyloggers are "just" malware, then the techniques you already have in place to avoid malware will keep you safe.

Hidden files

The amount of data that would be collected by recording every keystroke is no longer a reason it couldn't be done.

Let's say you're a prolific typist, and you type 100,000 keystrokes a day (that's over three keystrokes every second for a solid eight-hour work day). In a year, that adds up to 36 megabytes of data. Keep your computer for 10 years, and that's 360 megabytes. On today's hard disks, that's next to nothing. You'd probably never notice it.

So, are all your keystrokes being written to some hidden file? No.

But there is a kernel of truth here: there are hidden files on your machine.

- There are files marked with the "hidden" file attribute. The operating system itself often uses this attribute to hide some of its own files from casual observers. The system swap file, typically in the root of the C: drive, is a common example. These are easy to find, since both Windows File Explorer and the Command Prompt "DIR" command can be instructed to display files that have this "hidden" attribute.
- There are often "hidden" partitions on the hard drive. Many computer manufacturers, as well as recent versions of Windows, now use them to store their recovery data. These are easy to see with Window's built-in disk management tool or any partition management software.
- There's an obscure form of hidden data possible in files stored on a disk that's formatted using the NTFS file system. NTFS supports something called "alternate data streams". Not many people know about this feature, and it's difficult to detect if it's been used.
- Lastly, there are techniques, such as VeraCrypt's "Hidden Volume", which use various approaches to hiding data within other data.

As you can see, there's a potential for a lot of hidden information on your PC ...

... but none of them contain every keystroke you've ever typed.

Deleting files

We also need to understand how files are deleted, because that can result in a different type of "hidden" file: remnants of previously deleted files.

When a file is deleted, its contents are not actually removed. Instead, the space the file formerly occupied is marked as "available" for another file to be written to later. Until that overwrite actually happens, the original deleted information is still there.

This is the basis for many undelete and data-recovery utilities. It's also why most of those utilities recommend you stop using your disk if you accidentally delete something, so as to avoid overwriting the deleted area with something new. So just deleting something doesn't necessarily mean it's immediately or completely gone.

The article How Does Secure Delete Work? goes into this in more detail, including steps to take to make sure your deleted files' data is really gone.

Which brings us to DBAN.

Drive-wiping utilities

DBAN is a utility that securely erases *everything*. Without paying any attention to what's stored on it, DBAN overwrites the entire contents of a hard disk—every sector, whether in use or not.

Should you be worried?

In my opinion, as long as you follow the fundamentals of keeping your computer safe on the internet, the answer is clearly no. As I've said before, unless you're doing something illegal or secretive, you're just not that interesting.

When the time comes to dispose of hardware such as your disk drive, tools like DBAN are a fine way to make sure your private information is sufficiently erased.

⊙

Adjusting Windows 10 Privacy Settings

In an earlier *Ask Leo!* article, I covered adjusting the default Windows 10 privacy settings at the time you install or upgrade to it.

The key, as is true for all software installations, is to avoid the default "Express settings" option. Instead, always use custom settings, so as to expose the choices the setup program otherwise makes on your behalf.

But what if it's too late? What if you've already installed Windows 10, and want to adjust the settings after the fact?

I'll explore where those settings are kept and what you can change in your installed and running copy of Windows 10. Regardless of the decisions made at set-up time, you can always change your mind.

Windows 10 privacy settings

Click on the **Start** menu, and then click on **Settings**.

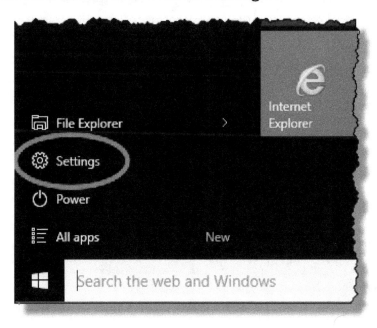

In the Settings application, click on the **Privacy** option.

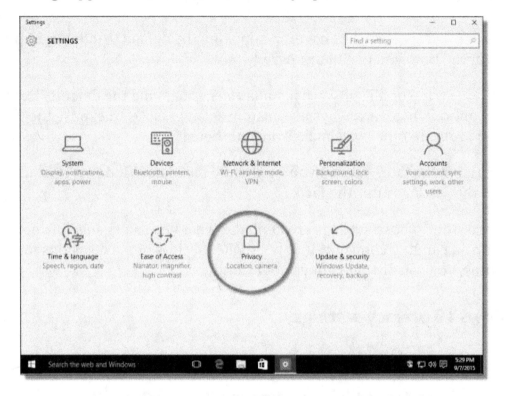

This will display a page with many of the privacy options we care about.

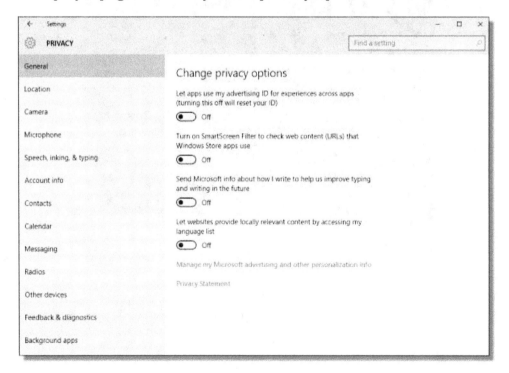

On the left, the "General" section of settings is selected by default, and several privacy options are displayed. Turn each on or off as you see fit. Click on **Location**, in the left-hand list, to bring up location-related settings.

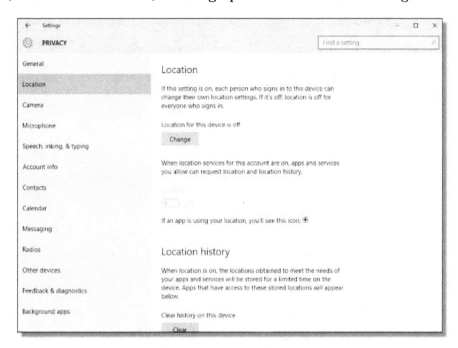

Once again, this displays a list of privacy settings you can elect to turn off or on as you see fit.

This is also an example of something easily overlooked: there's more to this list than fits on the screen. Click in the pane on the right and scroll down to expose more.

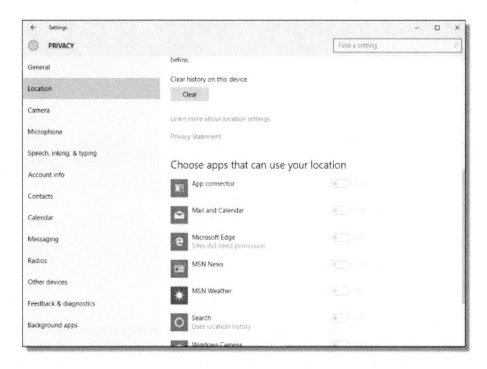

In fact, you may need to page down more than once to expose all the settings available in each section.

Repeat this for each of the sections listed in the left-hand pane. You'll find numerous privacy-related settings—many more, in fact, than were exposed at installation time. These allow finer control over specific aspects of Windows 10 privacy. Review each and decide which you want enabled.

In addition, in the "Background apps" section, you may be able to speed up your computer a little by disabling some background applications with privacy ramifications. Some of these apps simply may not apply to how you use your computer.

As many options as there are here, there are still more to check.

Control Panel settings

At least one setting mentioned in Windows 10 setup is in Control Panel.

There are many ways to launch Control Panel—perhaps the easiest is to type "control panel" in Windows Search, and click on Control Panel Desktop app when it appears.

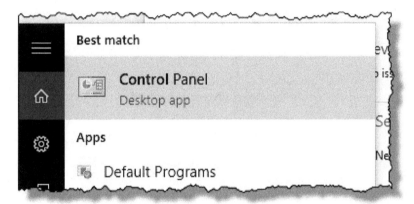

In Control Panel, click on **System and Security**, then **Security and Maintenance**, and then **Security** to expand the list of security-related options.

Here you'll find the Windows SmartScreen setting. While I recommend leaving it on for security, this is where you would turn it off if desired.

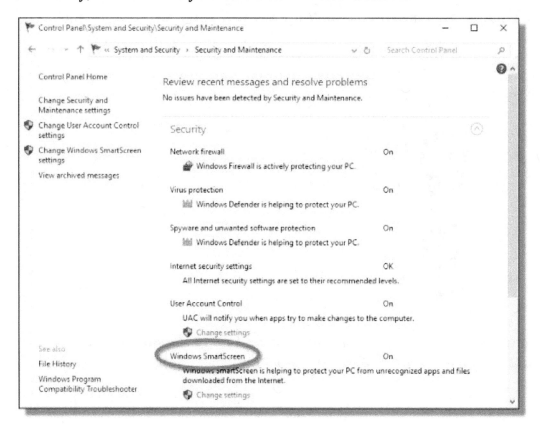

Interestingly, this seems unrelated, or perhaps only partially related, to a SmartScreen option we saw earlier in the Settings app, and possibly even unrelated to the SmartScreen setting listed in the Edge browser.

Microsoft Edge settings

Settings related to Edge, Microsoft's web browser, are naturally contained within the browser's own Settings page.

Fire up Edge, click on the <u>ellipsis</u> on the right end of the menu bar, and click on **Settings**.

Scroll down in the resulting setting pane, which will be displayed on the right side of the Edge window. This is another case where the fact that you can scroll down isn't necessarily obvious, but it's required to expose the additional settings we want.

Click on **View advanced settings**.

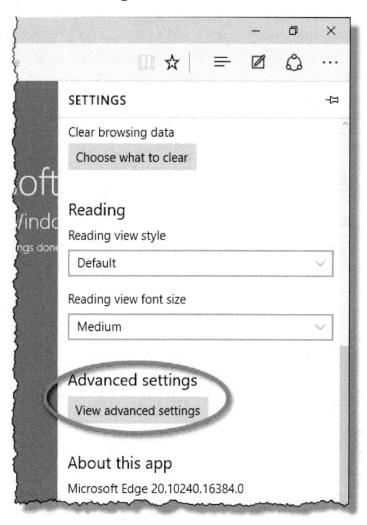

The resulting panel of options—once again, a longer list you need to scroll through to see in its entirety—includes several privacy-related options.

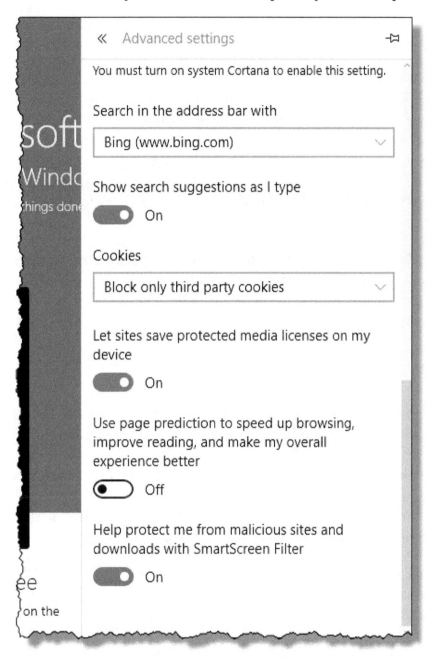

Scroll through the list, examine the various entries, and make sure they're set as you desire. My biggest recommendations are to block only third-party cookies, and to turn off "page prediction", which can cause additional internet traffic as Edge tries to guess which links to pre-load in case you click on them.

Additional settings

WiFi Sense, Microsoft's controversial attempt to make it easier to connect to your friends' password-protected WiFi hotspot, is covered in an article, How do I turn off Wi-Fi Sense (and what is it?).

It's important to remember that each application you run in Windows, regardless of Windows version, may have its own independent privacy-related settings. Internet Explorer 11, for example, includes yet another instance of the SmartScreen Filter setting, in addition to its own privacy and security-related settings. (In IE, click the gear icon, **Internet Options, Advanced**, and then scan through the list provided in *Settings*.)

On one hand, it might seem frustrating that you need to visit several places—the settings app, Control Panel, Edge, Internet Explorer, and so on—in order to review all the Windows 10 privacy settings. However, what we've been referring to as "Windows 10 privacy" is, in reality, a collection of the privacy settings of any number of different applications, in addition to the operating system itself.

Is this everything?

What's perhaps more frustrating about the privacy settings I've reviewed above is that we really don't know what else is being shared with Microsoft or third parties. The Privacy Policy we all agree to in order to install Windows 10 seems pretty vague and all-encompassing. While the settings we can adjust above (and perhaps more that I've overlooked) will control some of what is exposed, it's clear that in the long run, Microsoft has the ability, *and our permission*, to collect a lot of information about how we use Windows.

Some find this disturbing, because they fundamentally don't trust Microsoft, and resent the apparent requirement that this information be made available in order to run Windows 10.

I find it disturbing, not because I don't trust Microsoft—I actually do—but because it's such an obvious public relations nightmare, and to be blunt, a blunder. Microsoft could clear this up in an instant with three specific actions:
- Configure Windows 10 to share as little personal information as is practical by *default*. Then, perhaps, provide a reasonable incentive—either

a clear benefit or some kind of perk—to encourage customers to turn individual options on.

- Give users *clearer control*, perhaps with a dedicated privacy application, that more clearly spells out what type of information is collected, why, and exactly how it's used, with the option to turn each type of collection on or off.
- Be more *transparent* about data collection and use overall. This is really a generalization of the options provided in the previous point, but by being more clear, more transparent, and more specific about data collection and user privacy—perhaps even in some kind of independently verifiable way—Microsoft could turn all of this into a non-issue.

Until the unlikely day they choose to do so, the choice is up to you: use Windows 10[9] (or not), and if you use it, take the time to review the many privacy options that exist.

---

[9] It's possible that this discussion applies to Windows 7 and 8 as well, as recent Windows updates seem to increase the data collection happening in those versions of the operating system as well.

Every Application Adds Risk

When it comes to the operating system, our options are limited. There's really no choice: in order to use our device, we must use an operating system of some sort.

When it comes to the applications we install on our computers, we have more choice and more risk.

Every application adds direct risk

Every application you download and install on your computer, be it your desktop, laptop, tablet, or phone, is an opportunity for your security and privacy to be compromised.

We regularly give applications much broader permissions to operate on our information than they need. In Windows, most programs can read any file, whether they need to or not. For example, that desktop chess game you just downloaded has complete access to the financial spreadsheets stored elsewhere on your computer.

On the other end of the spectrum, some operating systems allow us to control permissions at a per-application level. For example, when installing an app on an Android-based device, you'll often be presented with a list of things to which the new application requires access.

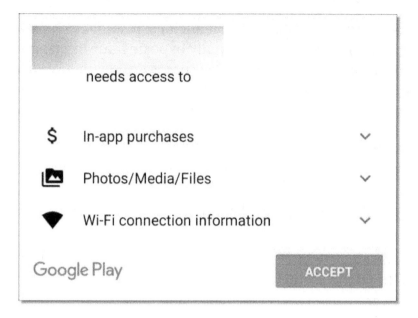

If we want the application at all, we must grant it all the permissions it requests. And that's exactly what most people, including myself, do: zip through the list of permissions requested as if it was a license agreement, and accept it all, without reading or considering.

Any application we install could be malicious. It could be explicitly malicious— meaning malware—or it could be less obviously malevolent, sharing more information with third parties than we realize, violating our assumptions of privacy.

As we'll see in a moment, as long as we take appropriate care, we can be relatively safe—but the possibility exists.

Every application adds indirect risk

Even the best-intentioned application includes risk, even if indirectly.

The program could have bugs. It could have errors or omissions that, in turn, could be leveraged by other, malicious software. It could "leak" our information unintentionally in ways third parties can intercept and collect.

Again, none of these risks are included purposefully, but rather as a side effect of oversight, poor design, poor coding, or other unintentional accidents.

A great example is Adobe Flash. It's not malicious. It's not *intentionally* allowing malware on our computers, or intentionally exposing our information to others. But (as of this writing) it has so many bugs, errors, and vulnerabilities that its mere presence on your machine—particularly if not updated regularly— increases the risk of other software leveraging those issues to do harm.

All software has bugs. Thus, all software comes with some risk that those bugs, once discovered, could be used by others in unintended ways.

Once again, it all comes back to trust

You and I can't be expected to understand all the details and nuances of software design and marketing. It's too complex and ever-changing.

Instead, we rely on third parties. Or, more correctly, we rely on our trust of third parties to either do or provide the right thing, or act as a resource to let us know when the right thing isn't happening.

This is why I so strongly warn against using download sites. The third parties involved—the download sites themselves—have a poor track record of providing software that can be trusted. Instead, I recommend you take the effort to locate the original vendor of whatever software you're looking for and download directly from the source.

Assuming, of course, you trust them.

I discuss ways of developing and evaluating trust in a previous chapter—What Does It Mean for a Source to be "Reputable"? That advice applies equally here. When it comes to the software you install on your machine—*any* software—you must weigh the benefits against the risks, and take care to make sure you trust the source.

Rule of thumb: don't install what you don't need

The most secure software of all is the software that isn't on your machine. If it's not there, it can't harm you.

I'm sure you know someone who constantly downloads and installs software on their machine. Be it a bevy of anti-malware tools, the latest games, or who-knows-what, their machine eventually becomes unstable—or worse, their online accounts get hacked as a result of malware that accompanied all those downloads…

… all for things they probably didn't really need.

Don't be that person. ☺

Think carefully before installing *any* software on your computer or other device. Even the most trustworthy and reputable software comes with side effects of some sort, and in the worst case, as we've seen, there's a risk of more malicious intent as well.

Make sure you need it. Make sure you trust the author. Make sure you get it from a source you trust.

And when in doubt, don't install it. You're safer that way.

Is anything safe?

All this sounds pretty daunting and perhaps even a little overwhelming. You might wonder if anything's ever safe.

The good news is that, for the most part, the software you need, from reputable sources, is generally not malicious, and largely well behaved. There are bad actors out there, of course, but keeping these basic rules of thumb in mind will generally allow you to be safe.

- Only install what you need.
- Install only reputable software from well-known sources.
- Download only from the vendor's own download site or instructions.

If you're at all concerned about security and privacy—and you should be—it's important to be aware and keep these rules in mind.

You'll have a much safer and more confident experience.

What Good is Incognito Mode?

I use incognito mode in my web browser to keep my online activities private. I mentioned that to a friend and he said it wasn't private at all. If he's right ... what's the point?

You're both right, and you're both wrong.

Incognito mode in Google Chrome, also referred to as "Private" or "InPrivate" in Firefox, Internet Explorer, Edge, and other browsers, protects your privacy *to a point*.

It's critical to know where that is, because beyond that point, Incognito does exactly nothing to keep you more private.

The Incognito line

The good news is that the point to which Incognito has impact, and beyond which it has no effect at all, is easy to understand.

Incognito affects only the information *stored in your computer*. Information stored or seen elsewhere is completely unaffected by Incognito.

Incognito does disable extensions

Entering Incognito mode varies based on browser, and there are multiple ways, but in Chrome, click on the ellipsis menu at the right end of the menu bar, and click on "**New incognito window**".

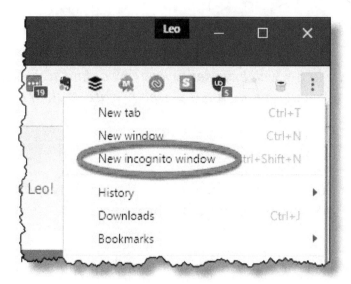

You can browse within that window normally, with the exception that your browser extensions may not be enabled in Incognito. If you need an extension to work in Incognito mode (for example, perhaps you need your password management software to be enabled) you'll need to enable it in the browser's extensions page. When you do, your browser may point out:

> **Warning**: Google Chrome cannot prevent extensions from recording your browsing history. To disable this extension in Incognito mode, unselect this option.

Browser extensions are one way your activities can be exposed, so disabling them by default makes a lot of sense. You can then choose which extensions you trust.

Incognito does delete history

The primary function of Incognito mode is that it doesn't save browsing history. This comes into play when you close the Incognito window or exit your browser. At that time, the following information about your Incognito activities is deleted:

- The history of websites you visited within Incognito windows (though any bookmarks you create will be retained).
- The history of files you've downloaded within Incognito windows (though the files themselves are left intact).
- The history of searches kept by the browser.
- Cookies left by the sites you've visited within Incognito windows.
- Form-fill information entered into Incognito windows that would normally be remembered for future auto-complete.
- The browser cache related to your Incognito activities.
- Any normal, non-Incognito windows are unaffected.

The idea is that once you exit an Incognito window, no trace of the activity that happened within that window is left *on your computer*.

Incognito does not hide what you're doing from others

Incognito only affects the data that is kept on your PC.

For example:
- Your network traffic is unaffected. Your ISP can still see what you're up to.
- The websites you visit have no idea you're incognito. They can still identify you by various means not limited to cookies, and they can still keep a record of your visit.
- The search history saved in the online account you might have with the search provider, like Google, is not affected.
- Any malware on your machine can see what you're up to.
- It's unlikely your browser performs a "secure" delete—meaning that the files it created might still be recoverable after your session.[10]

The bottom line is that Incognito (or Private or InPrivate) mode is great at preventing anyone with access to your computer from easily finding your activities there—but it does nothing to protect your online privacy.

It certainly shouldn't be considered as any kind of *absolute* privacy or security tool.

---

[10] This is *highly* implementation-dependent. Different browsers do things in different ways, ranging from not creating "files" at all, but keeping things in memory, to actually attempting a secure delete. The latter is not something I'd count on if it matters to you.

Google Remembers More than You Realize

The online services we choose to use are some of the least obvious and most ubiquitous collectors of our information.

None demonstrate this fact more clearly than Google.

As we go about out online activities, Google maintains a surprisingly detailed history of our activities. Most people don't realize just how detailed it is, or how long it's kept.

More interestingly, Google's one of the good players, as it actually exposes this history to us, and even allows us to clear it if we want.

My Activity

It's been called several things over the years, most commonly "web history". Today, it's referred to as "My Activity", since, as we'll see, it covers much more than web or search history.

Try it right now. Visit:

https://myactivity.google.com

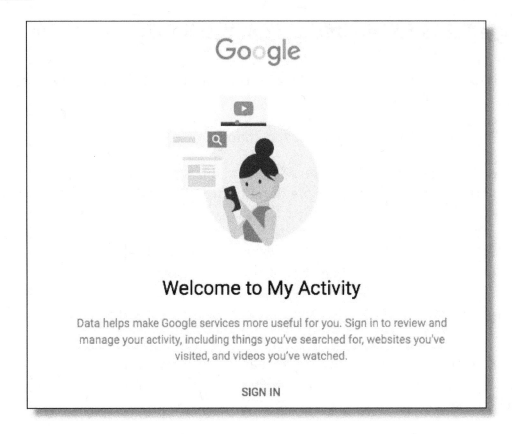

Sign in with your Google account.

A word about privacy

Near the top of the resulting page will be a statement from Google about who can see the information we're about to explore.

It's worth reviewing Google's privacy policy by clicking on the "Learn more" link. That'll take you to what I consider to be a somewhat "salesy" page that tells you why data collection is good for you. Near the bottom are the links to meatier pages:

The Ask Leo! Guide to Online Privacy askleo.com

Our commitments to your privacy and security:

We want you to understand what data we collect and use.

You have the controls to manage your privacy.

Your security comes first in everything we do.

We do not sell your personal information to anyone.

We help make the Internet safer for everyone.

My assumption is that Google can and will make any information it has on you available to law enforcement when compelled to do so. They have a record of fighting such requests, which is a very good thing, but I don't think it's safe to assume that they can and will win every such case in every jurisdiction.

Recent activity first

I logged in, and was immediately presented with my recent activity.

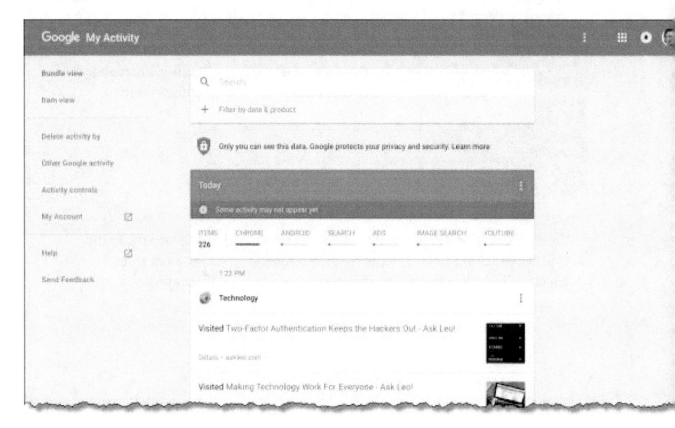

Google reported 226 items collected so far today.

- Chrome, my browser, was responsible for most of the items recorded.
- Android activity (from my phone) was included.
- Search is a separate category.
- Ads (It's unclear exactly what this refers to. I'd not clicked on any ads.)
- Image Search (I had been using earlier that day.)
- YouTube. I'd forgotten, but I'd viewed a YouTube video embedded on another site earlier in the day.

Clicking on any of those categories filtered the results.

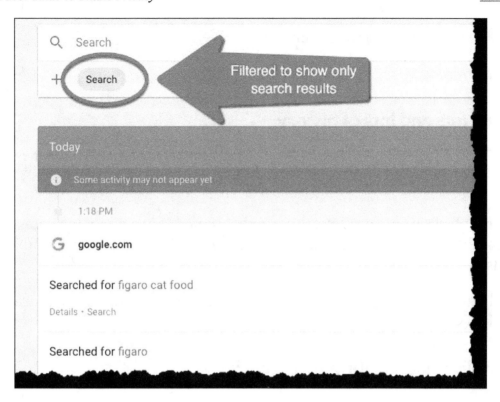

That's my search history immediately prior to beginning work on this article.[11]

The full list of products

I used my search history as my example above, but Google keeps records across almost all of its products. As of this writing, the full list you can filter on includes:

- Ads
- Android
- Assistant
- Books
- Chrome
- Developers
- Goggles
- Help
- Image Search
- Maps
- Maps Timeline
- News
- Play
- Play Music
- Search
- Shopping
- Video Search
- Voice & Audio
- YouTube

---

[11] Yes, Figaro, as in the cat food. Detailed research relating to the lyrics of "Bohemian Rhapsody", if you must know. 😊

That list will naturally change over time.

Speaking of time…

History: lots and lots of history

In addition to filtering by the "product" used, you can examine your information by date.

The user interface to specify dates is cumbersome.[12] My activity log dates back to at least 2006. That's a full decade of my online activity that Google has in its records.

Multiply that data by the number of Google users, and you have some idea of the breadth of data Google has on their hands.

Controlling and deleting your activity

On the left-hand side of the My Activity page (see above) are a couple of important links.

Activity controls lets you decide what information will and will not be collected at a high level. Data collection defaults to being "on". You can opt to turn off specific sections—like the Location History shown below—or you can turn all of them off, if you like.

---

[12] Cumbersome, as in awful. Abysmal. Horrific. Like they don't want you look back too far, because it involves a *lot* of clicking to get there.

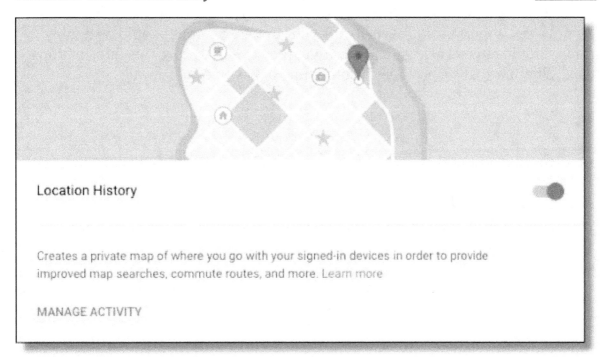

The assumption is that this turns off actual persistent data collection. Cynics might argue that the data might still be collected, and all we've done is restrict our own access to it. There's no way to know for sure.

Delete activity by allows you to delete the log of your activity by category or by date.

Is it time to panic?

My intent here isn't to scare you.

It's no secret that Google can, and obviously does, keep all this information. It's perhaps one of their biggest assets.

My purpose in pointing all this out to you is simply to raise awareness of how much information we "give away" in our daily lives online. Any online service we use has the ability to record our interactions with them. Some do. Some don't.

Google is upfront about it, making these details of their records easily accessible. As I said, in my opinion, they're actually one of the good guys when it comes to this kind of thing. Other companies and services don't publicize the information they keep, and I know of none that make it as easily reviewable.

By now, the importance of security for your Google account should be doubly clear. Should anyone else gain access to it, they could capture this information as well. Whether that's a problem is something only you can say.

Supercookies and Evercookies: Resistance is Futile

I just read an article talking about so-called "supercookies" and "evercookies"— *cookies* *which are supposedly impossible to delete, and left without the computer user's permission or even knowledge. What are "supercookies"? What are "evercookies"? And how can I protect my computer from them?*

I'll start out by saying that options to protect yourself from supercookies and evercookies are relatively limited, if effective at all.

Supercookies and evercookies are the result of a website owner's desire (or more often, the desire of the advertising networks used by websites) to accumulate data about computer users and the sites that they visit, even those users that disable or clear cookies in their browser regularly.

Bottom line: clearing cookies isn't enough—not nearly enough. There may be nothing that is.

Cookies

Cookies are part of the http protocol your web browser uses to request web pages, and web servers use to deliver them.

When you visit a site—say https://askleo.com—the web server may include, with the web page you see, a small text file containing some data you don't see. In a sense, your browser says, "Please give me https://askleo.com/", and the server replies, "Here's the page you requested, and here's some other data I'd like you to hold on to for me."

The data is called a "cookie". It can be *any* piece of information, and is stored somewhere on your computer by your web browser.

The next time your browser requests a page from that same site, it automatically sends the contents of that text file along with the request. To continue the analogy above, your browser might say, "I'd like to see https://askleo.com, and here's that bit of data you asked me to keep last time."

That's all a normal cookie is.

As I said, a cookie can be anything. The most obvious example is a unique number. The server makes up a completely new, unique number the first time it sends a cookie back to your computer. When your computer sends that number back on subsequent requests, the server knows the new request is coming from the same machine.

Cookies are most commonly used to <u>remember you're logged into a site</u> as you move from page to page. They're also used, as they are here on *Ask Leo!,* to remember you've been shown things like newsletter subscription offers, so you're not shown them again and again.[13]

Cookies also allow ad services to see what pages that machine has been visiting.

Supercookies

It's somewhat ironic, but what are being called "<u>supercookies</u>" aren't really cookies in the traditional sense, because they don't work in that browser-supported behind-the-scenes way.

A supercookie is just any *other* way of storing something unique from a website on your computer so it can be given back to the website the next time you visit.

The problem is, a supercookie is often difficult or impossible to clear.

Let's say the goal, as in the example above, is to assign your computer a unique number that can be "read" somehow during subsequent website visits to track that it's the same machine visiting each time.

There are perhaps a dozen or more different ways to do this that don't involve traditional cookies at all.

---

[13] Or at least for "a while". The newsletter offer popup on *Ask Leo!* should appear only every month or six. Unless, of course, you clear cookies.

Here are just two examples:

- Flash cookies: Many sites (still) use Adobe's Flash player, and as a result, it's (still) on most people's machines. So-called "Flash cookies" are data managed by the Flash player in a way very similar to regular cookies. Unfortunately, your web browser has no way to clear Flash cookies, though some tools, like CCleaner, can.
- Image hack: I call this a hack because it uses techniques never intended to achieve this goal. There are many possible variations, but as one example, let's say the web page you're visiting includes a small image hidden behind something. The colors values assigned to some pixels in the image, when combined, *are* the unique ID the web server uses. A small amount of Javascript or HTML5 coding elsewhere on the page then reads the pixel "colors" and reports back to the server the number found. On subsequent pages, the image—containing your unique number—comes from your browser's cache, rather than being downloaded anew.

These are just two examples; one is an intentional feature, and the other is an unintentional side effect of some clever programming. There are other approaches, and no doubt more that haven't been discovered or devised yet.

Evercookies

Let's assume a website uses all three of the techniques I've discussed so far: http cookies, Flash cookies, and the image hack.

It only takes one of them to work for your computer to be uniquely identified.

In fact, if any one of them work, the website can immediately reset the other two.

That's the concept behind what some have termed the "evercookie"—a technique that uses more like ten different approaches to identify your computer. If any one of those techniques work, the other nine can be reset, no matter how aggressively you clear them.

Clear your browser's http cookies? Evercookie techniques cause it to be immediately reset on your next visit, because perhaps a Flash cookie wasn't cleared. Cleared the Flash cookie? The cookie can be immediately reset on your next visit, because the image cache wasn't cleared. And so on for any number of techniques that could be used.

You get the idea. Evercookies turn this all into a game of whack-a-mole to keep your computer from being uniquely identified.

What I do

What do I do about all this?

Absolutely nothing.

I just don't believe browser-based tracking represents as <u>huge of a threat</u> as some seem to feel. Even supercookies and evercookies don't really worry me.

Most tracking isn't done at the individual level. No one cares that Leo Notenboom visited this site, and then that site, and then that site. What they do care about is that 1000 people did, and that those 1000 people should now see ads related to that site.

As I said, I don't care. At worst, it's an annoyance when I see the same ad everywhere I go on the internet.

Oh well.

If you want to do something…

I'll admit, though, as unlikely as I think it is, the technology certainly could be used to track me as an individual.

Some people simply don't appreciate their movements being tracked, even in a relatively benign, anonymous, aggregate way.

So how can you avoid it?

It's not easy. In fact, it's darned near impossible, if the websites you visit are determined to track you.

The only way is to be certain that nothing has been saved from a prior visit, and thus, there's nothing trackable being sent on subsequent visits.

The only guaranteed way to do that is to start with a completely fresh *computer* each time that you browse.

Harsh, I know.

The problem with the various techniques that create supercookies and evercookies is that we have no real confidence we can clear them all. Yes, browser extensions will come along to clear *more* of them, but as the evercookie example illustrates, a determined site need only have one technique that slips through to continue to track.

As I said, it's whack-a-mole, and the moles are winning.

There are two approaches to making the "start with a clean machine every time" approach slightly more palatable:

- Do your browsing within a virtual machine you *reset each time*.
- Use a live CD, such as the Ubuntu Live CD, that includes a web browser and saves nothing to your disk when it exits.

I don't believe "private" or "incognito" browsing will ever cover all possible tracking techniques.

The future

Even if so-called supercookies were completely outlawed, that law would only be valid in those countries that passed it, and even there, those that choose to flout the law would carry on.

In other words, legislation won't make the technology go away. If supercookies are outlawed, only outlaws will have supercookies.

I expect that the arms race will continue: browser features and add-ons will be developed to increase your privacy, and new tracking techniques will be developed to bypass them.

The good news is, I do believe various privacy watchdog groups will monitor most major sites and advertising networks—and perhaps law enforcement too, should legislation become a reality—and as a result, blatant violators will be taken to task.

I hope.

PRIVACY ISSUES: YOUR COMPUTER'S HARDWARE

Sometimes the Threat Is in the Hardware

Our computer's hardware—the circuits, chips, disks, memory, cables, and connectors—are all things we rarely think about when it comes to considering our privacy.

We would be wise to.

While not as easily compromised, since it requires some form of physical access, hackers know we take our hardware for granted, and when it comes to gaining intrusive access to our information, hardware represents a way in.

Hardware Keyloggers

A keylogger is typically a form of malware that resides on your computer, intercepting and recording all your keystrokes and sending them off to some malicious third party. Type in your username and password, and the keylogger intercepts and records it.

Keyloggers can also be present in hardware. A device inserted between your keyboard and computer can do exactly the same thing: record all keystrokes for transmission or later collection by that same malicious party.

Hardware keyloggers are less common, because they require physical access to the machine on which they're installed. Once installed, however, they're nearly impossible for the average computer user to detect. It doesn't matter what anti-malware tools are running, what operating system is installed, clean-installed, or booted from; the keylogger remains in place, recording your data.

There are two simple guidelines:
- Never use a public computer for anything in any way sensitive. Hardware keyloggers are most commonly found on public computers.
- Remember, "If it's not physically secure, it's not secure". If your computer is in a public or highly trafficked place, it's possible someone could add a hardware keylogger when you're not around.

Most people needn't worry about hardware keyloggers. As I said, they're rare, mostly because installation requires physical access to the machine.

But they definitely exist.

Public Charging

This is a relatively new, and to me, fascinating form of compromise.

You're on a trip, and your mobile phone's battery is running low, so you find a convenient charging station where you can plug in and top off the battery before you board your aircraft.

Unfortunately, that connection might provide more than power. The connection can actually include malicious hardware surreptitiously placed there by a hacker to leverage the data connection on your USB connection, examining the contents of your phone or even placing malware on it.

It's not common, but it can happen.

Fortunately, the solutions are simple.
- Never use a public USB connection for anything. You simply don't know what you're connecting to.
- Bring and use your wall-charger instead. Assuming you can find a wall outlet, this is a safe way to recharge your device.
- If you must, get and use a "data blocker", a device through which you make your USB connection, which in turns blocks any data connection attempts.

Always be careful what you connect your device to, be it your mobile phone, tablet, or laptop.

Other types of hardware compromise

These are significantly less common, but I want you to be aware of them.

BIOS infection

Technically, this is a software update, but it's to your hardware: the BIOS in your computer. It's nearly unnoticeable, and most anti-virus programs can't detect it.

You can reformat your machine completely, and the malware will still be there. The only solution, when this happens, is to re-flash your computer's BIOS.

If you think your BIOS has been infected, *it probably has not*. Once folks hear about this possibility, they're quick to jump to it as a conclusion when malware reappears after a clean rebuild of their machine. What happens much more frequently is that you reinstalled the same malicious software you had before.[14]

Cash Machine Skimmers

While not directly related to the technology you own, this relates to technology you *use*.

There are malicious devices that can be added to cash machines and credit card machines that read (or "skim") the information off the card you insert or swipe. When coupled with cameras that record the PIN you type to access your money, the thieves then have enough information to clone your card and access it themselves.

Security researcher Brian Krebs has apparently gotten into the habit of tugging on the card insertion point to make sure it's not one of these fake devices.

My advice? Tug if you like, but instead, only use your cards in devices in very public places, devices you're personally already familiar with, and at retailers with which you already have a relationship of trust.

Or stop by the bank in person; I'm sure they'd love to see you.

---

[14] Seriously. I've yet to see this actually happen to anyone who's come to me claiming it has.

The Security of "Things"

I am concerned about the recent denial of service attacks that have, evidently, been driven by huge numbers of compromised internet-connected devices. I don't want any of my devices to be part of that attack. All of my internet-connected devices are located behind my router (granted an old Linksys BEFSR81) and password protected. Is everything sufficiently "hidden" from internet attacks?? In any event, are strong passwords enough to prevent rogue access?

It's definitely a concern. Events have made two things excruciatingly clear:
- We're connecting more and more non-traditional devices to the internet.
- Security on those devices is, apparently, abysmal.

So how do you protect yourself from being part of the problem? Well, as with so many things, there's no clear or absolute answer—but I do have a couple of ideas.

The internet of things

The term that's been flying around of late is "the internet of things".

It's nothing special, really. It's not another network, it's not something super secret or super complex. In fact, you may already have devices that are part of it.

All "the internet of things" really refers to is non-traditional devices connected to the internet. And by "non-traditional", I mean anything you wouldn't think of as a computer.

That's really all it is.

Your PC, laptop, smartphone, and tablet are all things we conceptualize as computers. Even your printers and gaming consoles are easily understood to be computers on the inside. Naturally, your router and other networking devices are also what we'd call "traditional" things connected to the internet.

On the other hand, so-called "smart" TVs, security cameras, light switches, light bulbs, refrigerators, washing machines, and perhaps even toasters[15] are being

---

[15] One concept toaster gets the daily weather forecast from the internet and burns it onto your toast.

connected to the internet for a variety of purposes. Whether you think it's the best thing since remotely-controlled sliced bread, or the silliest thing you've ever heard, the internet is being used in new and novel ways for all sorts of things we'd never considered before.

That whole "never considered" thing is actually part of the problem.

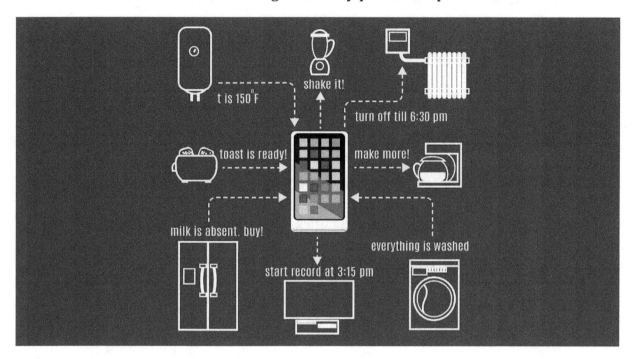

The (lack of) security of things

Who would want to hack a light bulb?

That appears to be exactly the kind of thing that appears to be happening in distributed denial of service (DDOS) attacks.

Hackers aren't interested in playing with your lighting. They are interested in using the tiny computer inside your light bulb (or other internet-connected smart device) for their purposes elsewhere on the network.

Computer in your light bulb?

Indeed. The easiest—indeed, the cheapest—way to make a device connect to the internet is through a general purpose interface that is, for all intents and purposes, a computer. It may not run Windows (though it might be running

Linux), and it may not have as many functions as your desktop computer, but it's a computer nonetheless. The protocols used to connect to the internet, as well as interface with the device itself, are complex enough that a fair amount of computing power is required to make it happen.

And as we all know, computing power is dirt cheap these days.

Sadly, security is not. Security requires forethought. What we're finding is that security is often an afterthought.

At best.

What can you do?

Being behind a router is the first step. The problem is, it's probably a step you've already taken. In fact, it's probably a step most people have taken, and yet internet-connected devices are being hacked on a regular basis anyway.

The single most important step? *Change the default password* on every internet-connected device you own. Apparently, a large number of hacks have been simply that: attackers discover the device through some means, and are able to log in to the administration of the device, because the owner never changed the default password.

In this case, it seems just about anything other than the default will cause attackers to move on, looking for a vulnerable device elsewhere. Use a strong password anyway, to future-proof yourself from the day when hackers get more aggressive. It's very likely, for example, that devices do *not* have brute force log-in protection, and could allow an attacker to try to log in using every possible password.

What you can't fix ...

What you can't fix is bad design[16].

---

[16] I was tempted to title this section "You can't fix stupid", but that's not fair. Most of the decisions that have led to this situation aren't as much about stupidity as they are about time pressure, ignorance, and failing to learn the lessons of the past.

There are so many ways these inexpensive internet-connected devices can communicate, there's a near endless supply of things that could go wrong.

For example, many devices use unencrypted connections to reach out to the internet, since https takes more work. That means it's possible for hackers to see, and perhaps intercept, traffic to and from the devices behind your router. It's possible that a single compromised device could expose other devices behind your router. Or it could mean nothing at all, depending on the device.

Unfortunately, aside from paying attention to news reports listing specific brands, devices, and models, there's no practical way to know if your devices are involved.

Aside from disconnecting it from the internet, it's almost impossible to know whether or not your refrigerator is helping to take down websites.

What I do

As geeky as I am, I have surprisingly few "internet of things" things. Don't get me wrong—I have many devices connected to the internet, but they mostly fall into the category of "traditional" devices. Computers, laptops, mobile phones—even Amazon's Echo—all qualify as more-or-less full-fledged computers.

I do have so-called "smart" TVs. It didn't take long for me to feel that they weren't smart enough; in the interest of preserving internet bandwidth—for a long time a scarce commodity here—I left them disconnected. I notice no function or feature loss by using them without connectivity.

While some of the features and functionality of newer devices is appealing, it's not appealing enough—to me—to make it worthwhile to buy something just because it can connect to the internet. If I were building a home from scratch, I'd probably build more in, but as it is, each device is a case-by-case basis, and the connectivity just doesn't add that much value to the way we use our devices.

That may change over time, as we learn new ways to make use of that connectivity. Hopefully, in the meantime, we'll also learn how to make them secure.

What is frustrating

What's particularly frustrating for internet technologists is that we've been here before.

All the lessons we've learned over the years from technologies like Bluetooth (originally very insecure), wireless keyboards, and even the Wi-Fi protocols we use every day have been, for the large part, ignored by the manufacturers of these new internet-connected devices. They opted for cheap and fast-to-market over keeping things secure[17].

So we learn the lessons again.

We hope.

⊙

---

[17] It's actually a complex equation. Consumers don't care about their refrigerator being secure, as long as it works. It's a hard sell to convince consumers to pay something extra, or wait a little longer, so their fridge doesn't also participate in the take-down of some random site on the internet.

Walking Away from Your Computer

If it's not physically secure, it's not secure.

That's a phrase I've used in several articles on security, but I've decided it deserves its own dedicated discussion as it applies to privacy.

You can have the best security software. You can be the greatest at identifying and avoiding phishing and other attempts to trick you into downloading malware. You can have the greatest, strongest passwords, doubly secured with two-factor authentication....

... and it's all for naught the moment someone else gets their hands on your machine.

The friends and family plan

This scenario is all too familiar.

You feel safe at home, so you don't bother locking your computer or taking other security precautions. It's just you and the people you trust, right? Be it a spouse, roommate, or a good friend over for dinner, there doesn't seem to be a reason to take special precautions.

That's exactly how I roll. If you walk into my home, there's a good chance you can walk into my office and start typing away at my desktop computer.

But I often hear from folks who shouldn't have felt quite so secure in their surroundings. Be it a friend pulling a prank by taking a photo with your phone, or a soon-to-be ex taking revenge on your online accounts, or a child just wanting to play with your shiny toy, unlimited access to the technology you have lying around isn't the safest or most secure approach to take.

I'm fortunate in that I feel appropriately secure *for my situation*. What matters most is that I've thought about it on more than one occasion, rather than just assuming I'm safe or not giving it any thought at all. Usually folks who run into problems fall into that latter camp, having given little or no thought to whether they consider their home (or workplace) "safe".

I'll just be a second

I began writing this in a local Starbucks—a place most folks consider anything but a "secure" location. Using the coffee shop's Wi-Fi through a VPN, I secured my internet connection, and my laptop never left my sight.

The gentleman next to me, on the other hand, was working on something and then ... left. I didn't check to see if he was just picking up a refill or making room for more; the fact was, he *walked away* from his *open* and *running* laptop (and a few other belongings). He returned after a couple of minutes and resumed his work.

I know if you hang out at your local coffee shop or Wi-Fi-enabled eatery often enough, it can start to feel like home. But it's not. You might assume that the other mobile techie nearby is a "friend" who'll keep an eye on your things for a few seconds, but that's a very bad assumption. You might assume that as long as it's within eyesight, nothing bad will happen.

There are *so many ways* this can go wrong.

The most common result is theft. But walking away, even for a few seconds, opens the door to everything that unfettered access to your device allows.

Inspect this

Also consider the privacy implications of inspection when crossing international borders.

Depending on where you live, where you're going, and the current political climate, any devices you take with you may be subject to inspection. That inspection could require you to provide full access to the contents of the device.

This is actually quite controversial, particularly in the U.S., and there are arguments and assumptions on both sides of the issue. What's important here is to realize that:
- This could happen
- It involves full access
- It's subject to the laws of the country you are travelling to, which may be radically different than what you're used to.

It may be something most people needn't be too concerned about, but it's important to be aware of and consider this possibility before traveling.

Thieves? Yeah, but…

Many people consider theft to be the biggest thing to worry about.

If your data isn't backed up and would disappear along with your computer, that might be true. But if you've been backing up appropriately, theft is *generally* an inconvenience and not actually a disaster.

It's my belief that the majority of burglary and opportunistic theft is all about the hardware, not the data stored on it. Most thieves simply aren't that technically savvy, and are more interested in turning a quick profit by selling the hardware. Unless you've been specifically targeted for some reason, your data is probably not that interesting, and will likely never be noticed.

Of course, "likely" isn't never. You should still take precautions. When someone steals your equipment, they have everything on it. Depending on their level of expertise (or that of the person they sell it to), and the preparations you've made (or haven't), they could once again have access to everything.

I do take steps, some of which I'll outline below, and should anything ever be stolen, I'll be changing passwords, of course. It's just not the first thing I think of when securing my equipment.

Steps to take

When it comes to physical security, there are a variety of steps you can take, but the most important is simply to keep it mind.

Encrypt, encrypt, encrypt

In recent years, I've become a big fan of whole-disk encryption. I use it not only on any laptops I travel with, but also on my desktop computer.

Think of whole-disk encryption as password-protecting everything. Without the correct password (be it a real password, or your system log-in credentials), the information on your hard disk is simply inaccessible. As long as the machine is not running, or has been logged off, whoever has physical access to it simply can't get at anything. Period.

Particularly if you're in a situation where theft is a real concern, such as travel, whole-disk encryption is the first step to keeping your information secure. Similarly, make sure to enable encryption on any mobile devices that support it.

Important: remember that if, for some reason, you can't log in to your own machine (or forget the password), you, too, *will be unable to access the data* contained on the disk. It's critical you have a separate backup, kept secure in some other fashion. Make sure also to take advantage of any backup options, like a recovery key, offered by the encryption technology you use.

Log out

Yes, having to log in to your machine is an inconvenience. But by not having a login, you've made it a trivial matter for anyone to walk up to your computer at any time and access its contents, running or not.

Minimally, make sure a password is required to access your computer, and use a screen saver that requires a password be specified to regain access after some period of inactivity.

Similarly, make sure your mobile device has a PIN code[18]. Configure an appropriate time-out, after which the device requires the code to access the device's contents.

For bonus points, consider getting into the habit of locking your computer or device when you walk away (keyboard shortcut: Windows key + L).

---

[18] It's unclear that a fingerprint unlock is sufficient. At a minimum, it seems to be legal to require that you present your fingerprint to unlock a device, as opposed to disclosing a PIN code.

Take your laptop when you pee

I'll be blunt: if I'm at the coffee shop and need to use the restroom, my laptop comes with me. I do not trust it away from my sight. Honestly, even walking a couple of dozen feet away to get sweetener for my coffee makes me uncomfortable, even though the device is within eyesight.

This is true for any public place you take and use your devices, including airports, libraries, and schools. It even applies when at the home of your latest new acquaintance or friend-of-a-friend. At a minimum, make sure the device is locked if you do walk away.

Lock the doors

I hear fairly regularly from individuals who've had their information compromised by their roommates or roommates' friends. In situations like this, one of the most common solutions is to lock your device.

Not with software (though that's good too)—with hardware.

Get a lock for the room containing your computer, or find some other form of *physical* security to prevent access or theft.

Make travel plans

Travel can be complex, depending on where you're going and what you need to take with you.

At one extreme, the Electronic Frontier Foundation has some ideas for individuals traveling internationally that could include traveling with only pristine devices that contain no sensitive data whatsoever, and relying on cloud access for the information you need.

At a more practical level, the single most important thing you can do is plan for your device(s) to be lost. Not only is losing a device when traveling frighteningly common, preparing for the possibility also readies you for theft. Encrypting, backing up, logging out, and making a habit of all the items I've discussed above are key to traveling safely and keeping our digital lives secure.

There are times, intentionally or otherwise, where our devices will be out of our control and potentially in someone else's hands. It's at those times it's important to remember the most basic rule of all:

If it's not physically secure, it's not secure.

8 Steps to a Secure Router

The topic is an important one: how do you make sure you have a secure router? As your firewall, it's your first line of defense against malware trying to get at your computer from the internet.

You'll want to make sure there aren't big gaping holes. And sadly, very often and by default, there are.

Here are the most important eight steps to a more secure router.

My router versus your router

I have to start with a caveat: there are hundreds, if not thousands, of different routers. Different brands and different models with differing capabilities, power, and, of course, at differing cost.

Most importantly, they have different administration interfaces.

What that means is, I can't tell you exactly how to make changes to your router, step-by-step. The concepts I'll cover apply to almost all consumer-grade routers, and I'll be using an old and popular LinkSys BEFSR81 router, and a LinkSys WAP54G access point, as examples.

You'll need to "translate" the examples to the equivalent settings on your own router or access point. Make sure you have access to the documentation that came with your router, or locate the user's manual online.

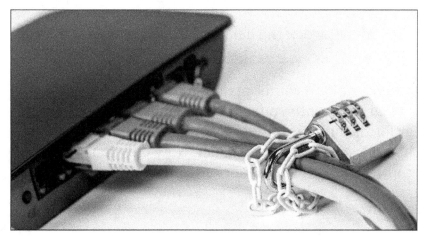

Already we see a common difference: you may well have a single device that combines both the router and wireless access point. You probably refer to it as simply your "router". In reality, there are two separate devices—a router that deals with network access, and a wireless access point that provides your Wi-Fi connectivity—that happen to be housed in a single box. In my case, they're in separate boxes.

1. Change the default password

If you do nothing else to secure your router, *change the default password*. Change it to be something <u>long and strong</u>. If your router supports it, a pass*phrase* of three or more words might be ideal.

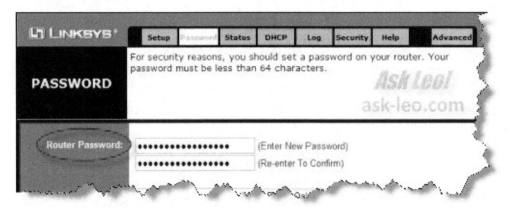

The reason for this is quite simple: it's a common gaping security hole.

For many years, almost every router and access point from the same manufacturer was shipped with the same default password. For LinkSys, if your login is a blank username and a password of "admin", as outlined in its manual, then anyone and everyone knows it. Anyone can log in to your router and undo any or all of the rest of the security steps we're about to take.

Then, any malware that takes advantage of the default passwords on routers can make changes without your knowledge.

Fortunately, most (though sadly, not all) router manufacturers have gotten smarter. If the instructions that came with your router included checking a sticker on the actual router for the admin password, and that looks like a strong password, then the security hole is significantly smaller. Now only those people who can walk up to your router and look at that sticker can get in.

I'd change the password anyway.

2. Disable remote management

"Remote Management" is a feature that allows your router to be administered from anywhere out on the internet.

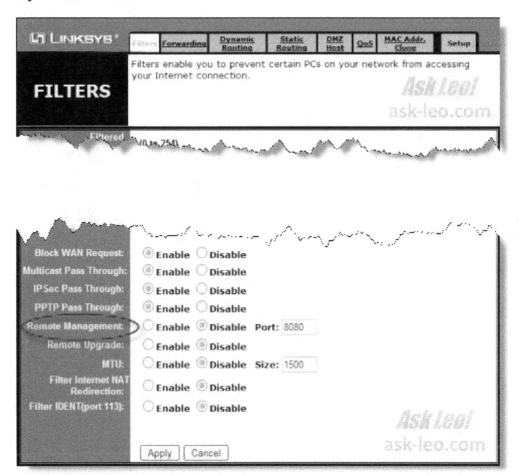

While this setting (coupled with a *very* strong password) might make sense for a handful of people[19], for most folks there's absolutely no need to administer the router from anywhere but the local machines connected to it.

Make sure the remote management setting is off.

---

[19] Some ISPs will insist on this, but they'll also prevent you from administering your own router as well. More common is a scenario where you're responsible for supporting someone else's network—say that of a friend or family. Remote administration can be helpful in a case like that. Even so, I'd think twice about setting it up, and insist on an exceptionally secure password if you do.

3. Turn off Universal Plug and Play

Universal Plug and Play (UPnP) is a technology that allows software running on your machine to configure services like port forwarding (a way of allowing computers outside your network to access your local computers directly) without you having to go in and administer the router manually.

It seems like a good idea, right?

Nope. Turn it off.

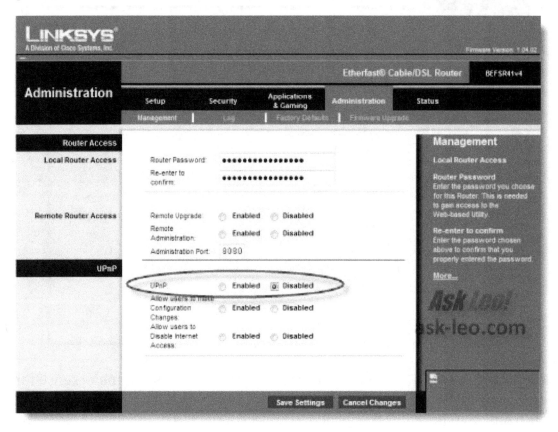

It turns out that malware can also be UPnP aware, and can make malicious changes to your router without your involvement or awareness.

(Note: UPnP is unrelated to Windows "Plug and Play" hardware detection; it's just an unfortunate collision of similar names.)

4. Add a WPA2 key

It's time for another password, this time to secure and encrypt your wireless connection.

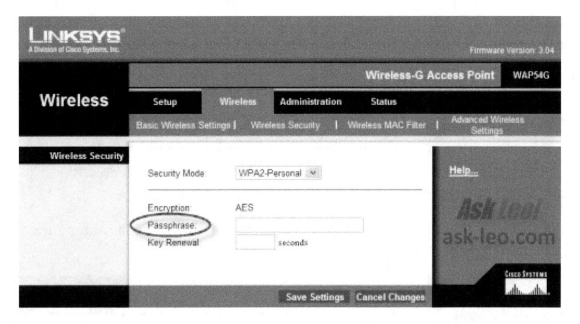

First, use WPA2, *not WEP*. WEP encryption turns out to be very easily crackable[20], and even WPA (without the 2) has been shown to be vulnerable.

Second, just as you did for the router's administration password, select another good, secure key/password/passphrase (the terms are roughly interchangeable here). You only need to enter it once here, and once on each machine allowed to connect to your wireless network.

Having a strong WPA2 key ensures that only machines you allow on your network can see your network, your traffic, and your router.

5. Disable WPS

WPS, or Wi-Fi Protected Setup, doesn't live up to its name—it's not very "protected" at all.

---

[20] It's essentially like having no encryption at all.

WPS was intended as a way to make setting up a protected Wi-Fi network easy. WPS would, with the push of a button, set up Wi-Fi encryption between the router and clients that supported it.

The problem with WPS is that the protocol is flawed in such a way that it is vulnerable to a brute force attack. A malicious entity within range can force their way onto your network bypassing any encryption keys you set up.

WPS is enabled by default on many routers. Turn it off.

6. Turn off logging

This has less to do with configuring a secure router, and more to do with maintaining your privacy.

This is also about making sure logging is still turned off, since if a router supports any kind of logging at all, it'll likely be off by default.

Disable the logging, and no information will be kept on the router, or sent to any other machine. This should also clear any log the router has.

It's worth pointing out that most consumer-grade routers do not have the capacity to actually keep complete logs themselves. If they keep anything, it will only be a shorter, partial log. When enabled, some will offer to send the log to one of the computers on your network for storage. Simply disabling logging will not erase any logs stored elsewhere.

7. Secure your router physically

As we've already seen, even if the default administrative password is unique to your device, it's still visible to anyone with physical access to the router who can see the sticker on which it's printed.

In fact, your secure router may not be secure at all if anyone can just walk up to it.

All of your router's security settings can be reset in a flash if someone has physical access to the device. Almost all routers have a "reset to factory defaults" mechanism (typically by holding a reset button for a certain amount of time). If someone can walk up to your router and do that, all the security settings you've just enabled may be instantly erased.

Only you can judge whether or not you need this extra level of physical security, but make sure to consider it.

8. Check for firmware updates

Routers (and access points) are really just small computers dedicated to a single task: handling network traffic. Normally the software—referred to as "firmware", since it's stored within the device's hardware—is solid and just works.

Unfortunately, security vulnerabilities are sometimes discovered, requiring you to update your router's firmware to stay secure. This usually involves downloading a file for your specific router, and then using its administration interface to install the update. Some routers can fetch and install the update directly. Either way, the update is a manual step you need to take.

Checking to see if there's a firmware update for your router is also a manual step. Some routers will perform the check at the push of a button in the administration interface. If not, you'll need to visit the manufacturer's support site, look for information pertaining to your specific model, and determine if a newer version of the firmware is available.

Two steps that aren't steps

People often make two additional suggestions for Wi-Fi that are not steps that improve security at all. In fact, they may harm security by providing a false sense of added security.

The first is MAC address filtering. I discuss this in more detail in the *Ask Leo!* article Is MAC address filtering a viable wireless security option?, but the bottom line is that like a cheap padlock, MAC address filtering only keeps out honest people. If someone wants to access your network, MAC address filtering is easily bypassed.

The second is turning off SSID broadcast on wireless networks. Even when not being broadcast, the SSID is still visible—unencrypted—in the packets of traffic sent to and from the router. Disabling the broadcast does nothing to prevent someone with the skills from easily discovering it. I discuss this in more detail in Does changing or disabling the broadcast of my wireless SSID make me more secure?

When it comes to Wi-Fi, putting a WPA2 password on the connection is (as of this writing) your best security measure.

Using Open Wi-Fi Safely

It can be absolutely safe to send and receive email from a coffee shop, or any other location that provides unsecured or "open" Wi-Fi. In fact, I do it all the time.

But you do have to follow some very important practices to ensure your safety.

Turn on the firewall

Fortunately, firewalls are "on" by default in most operating systems.

However, when you're at home, you may use your router as your firewall, and keep any software firewall on your machine disabled. That works well, as the router stops network-based attacks before they ever reach your computer... while you're at home.

When you're on an open Wi-Fi hotspot, or connected directly to the internet via other means, that software firewall isn't redundant. In fact, it's critical.

Make *sure* the firewall is enabled before connecting to an open Wi-Fi hotspot. Various network-based threats could be present on an untrusted connection, and it's the firewall's job to protect you from exactly that.

Secure your desktop email program

If you use a desktop email program, such as Microsoft Office's Outlook, Windows Live Mail, Thunderbird, or others, you *must* make certain it is configured to use SSL/secure connections for sending and downloading email.

Typically, that means that when you configure each email account in your email program, you need to:
- Configure your POP3 or IMAP server for accessing your email using the SSL, TLS, or SSL/TLS security options, and usually a different port number.
- Configure your SMTP server for sending email using SSL, TLS, or SSL/TLS security options, and usually a different port number, such as 26, 465, or 587 instead of the default 25.

The exact settings, and whether or not this is even possible, depends entirely on your email service provider; you'll need to check with them to determine the correct settings. How you configure these settings, of course, depends on the email program you use.

With these settings, you can feel secure downloading and sending mail using an open Wi-Fi hotspot.

Secure your web-based email

If you use a web-based email service like Gmail, Outlook.com, Yahoo, or others via your browser, you must make sure that it uses an http**S** connection and that it keeps on using that http**S** connection throughout your email session.

Fortunately, most of the major email services have moved to making https the standard (and sometimes the only) connection method.

Accessing email using a plain http connection might well be the source of many open Wi-Fi-related hacks. I expect people simply log in to their web-based email service without thinking about security; as a result, their username and password are visible to any hackers in range who care to look.

Be careful. Some services use https only for your login, which is insufficient, as your email conversations thereafter could be viewed by others. Other services may "fall out" of https, reverting to unsecure http without warning.

Secure all your other online accounts

Any and all web-based (aka "cloud") services that require you to log in with a username and password should either be used only with https from start to finish, or should be avoided completely while you're using an open Wi-Fi hotspot.

With more and more services being provided online, this is getting to be a larger problem.

Using "the cloud" is a great way to manage your digital life from wherever you may be, but one of the key problems remains security. Using https is critical to that security when you're out and about.

Use a VPN

This one's for the road warriors. You know them: the folks who are always traveling and online the entire time, often hopping from coffee shop to coffee shop in search of an internet connection as they go.

A VPN, or Virtual Private Network, is a service that sets up a securely encrypted 'tunnel' to the internet and routes all of your internet traffic through it. Https or not, SSL/secure email configuration or not, all of your traffic is securely tunneled, and no one sharing that open Wi-Fi hotspot can see a thing.

This service typically involves a recurring fee. As I said, they're great for road warriors, but probably overkill for the rest of us, as long as we follow the other security steps described above.

Use different passwords

Finally, it's important to keep your account passwords different from each other and, of course, secure.

That way, should one account be compromised by some stroke of misfortune, the hackers won't automatically gain access to your other accounts. Remember, even when you use an open Wi-Fi hotspot properly, a hacker can still see the sites you're visiting, even though they cannot see what you are sending to and from that site. That means they'll know exactly what sites to target.

Consider not using free Wi-Fi at all

As I said, it can be safe to use open Wi-Fi, but it's also very easy for it to be unsafe.

A very common and solid solution is to use your phone instead.

While it is technically possible, a mobile/cellular network connection is significantly less likely to be hacked. In fact, I use this solution heavily when I travel.

Most mobile carriers offer one or more of the following options:
- Use your mobile device. Many phones or other mobile devices, such as iPhones, iPads, Android-based phones, and others are quite capable email and web-surfing devices, and typically do so via the mobile network. (Some can also use Wi-Fi, so be certain you're using the mobile broadband connection for this option to avoid the very security issues we're discussing.)
- Tether your phone. Tethering means you connect your phone to your computer—usually by a USB cable, but in some cases, via a Bluetooth connection—and the phone acts as a modem, providing a mobile broadband internet connection.
- Use a dedicated mobile modem. Occasionally referred to as "air cards", these are USB devices that attach to your computer and act as a modem, providing a mobile broadband internet connection, much like tethering your phone.
- Use a mobile hotspot. In lieu of tethering, many phones now have the ability to act as a Wi-Fi hotspot themselves. There are also dedicated devices, such as the MiFi, that are simple dedicated hotspots. Either way, the device connects to the mobile broadband network and provides a Wi-Fi hotspot accessible to one or more devices within range. When used in this manner, these devices act as routers and must be configured securely, including a WPA2 password, so as not to be simply another open Wi-Fi hotspot susceptible to hacking.

I travel with a phone capable of acting as a hotspot. I find this to be the most flexible option for the way I travel and use my computer.

Don't forget physical security

Laptops are convenient because they're portable. And because they're portable, laptops are also easily stolen.

Unfortunately, it only takes a few seconds for an unattended laptop to disappear. That's one reason I never leave mine alone: even if I need to make a quick trip to the restroom, the laptop comes with me. There's just no way of knowing that absolutely everyone around is completely trustworthy.

In that same vein, I also prepare in case my laptop does get swiped. Specifically, that means:

- My hard drive is encrypted.
- My sensitive data is stored in folders that are encrypted using BoxCryptor, which is not mounted unless I need something.
- LastPass is set to require a password re-prompt after a certain amount of inactivity.
- I have two-factor authentication enabled on as many accounts as support it, including LastPass.
- I have tracking/remote wiping software installed.

Computer theft and recovery is a large topic that's only tangential to using open Wi-Fi hotspots. Clearly, though, if you are a frequent user of assorted open hotspots in your community or when you travel, a little attention to theft prevention and recovery is worth it as well.

Security and convenience are always at odds

As you can see, it's easy to get this stuff wrong, since doing it securely takes a little planning and forethought.

But it's important. If you're not doing things securely, that guy in the corner with his laptop open could be watching all your internet traffic on the Wi-Fi connection, *including your account username and password* as they fly by.

When that happens, you can get hacked.

Fortunately, with a little knowledge and preparation, it's also relatively easy to be safe.

How Do I Protect Myself from Other Computers on My Local Network?

We're a family where the adults use the Internet for serious reasons, and we can't take a chance on having our children screw things up - intentionally or by accident. How should we set up our home network?

Normally, we think of threats as being "out there" on the internet. The problem is that sometimes the threat is nearby, right in our own home.

This article was originally titled "How Do I Protect Myself from My Children?" On reflection, though, it's not just the kids you need to worry about; it's just about any device you connect to your network: the computer your friends bring over, the "internet of things" enabled device you purchase, the smart TV ... and yes, sometimes the computer belonging to a precocious child.

The good news is, you can protect yourself. You just have to look at your network a tad differently.

Who do you trust?

First, we need to group the computers in your home into distinct buckets:
- Computers you trust. These are the computers you control, and can safely assume are being used by individuals who understand the basics of keeping a computer safe on the internet.
- Computers you don't trust. These are the computers used by people who are less computer savvy, don't understand safety, and are likely to do things that they shouldn't, resulting in frequent infections of malware.
- Devices you're unsure of. In recent years, more and more devices are getting connected to our internet to create the so-called "internet of things". We're coming to realize these devices are built with security as an afterthought, if at all.

To protect one bucket from the others, we need to split the network somehow, which might be easy if your router supports it, or slightly more difficult if not. On top of that, we also need to talk about how the "Internet of Things" and software firewalls affect what we do.

Split the network using guest access

One approach is to carve your local network into two: a trusted and an untrusted network.

Routers protect you from the internet: the threats that are "out there". A more simplistic way to think of it is simply this: one side of a router is trusted—the LAN (Local Area Network) into which you plug in your computers—and the other side, the WAN (Wide Area Network), or internet side, is not.

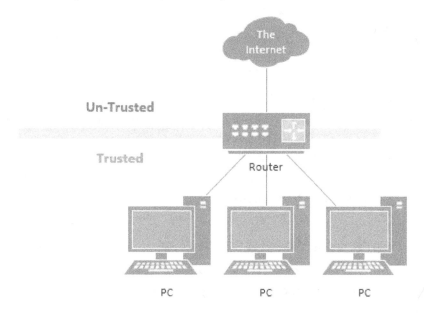

The router protects the trusted side from the untrusted side by preventing incoming connections: only connections that originate from the trusted side can be made across the router.[21] In other words, only information your computer *asks* for comes across the connection. Malicious attempts to get into your computer from out in the wilds of the internet are blocked.

Some modern consumer routers include what is called "guest access". This creates two local networks isolated from one another.

---

[21] Even connections that *look like* they've been initiated by an external source (say a software update) are actually created by software on the PC reaching out to the remote server on the internet.

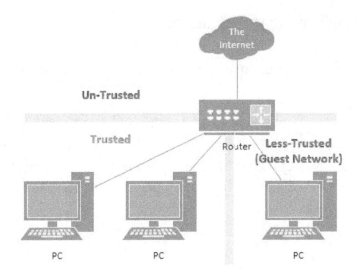

Guest access protects the trusted side from the less-trusted, as no connections can be made between the two, while protecting them both from the internet.

Unfortunately, guest access is usually restricted to wireless connections. That means if you have a wired connection, like that of your kid's computer in their bedroom, you may not have this option.

Split the network by getting a second IP

In our last example, we set up two local networks isolated from one another by virtue of the split that happens at the router. This works well, as the router not only splits the network but allows you to share the single IP address assigned to you by your ISP.

Of course, with your ISP's help, you can set up two, actual, distinct networks.

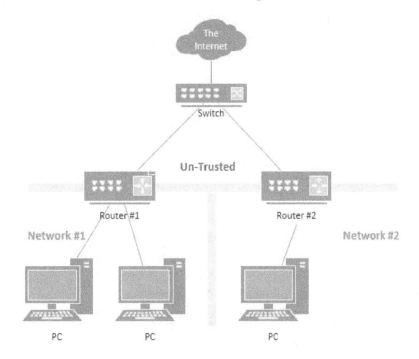

All you need from your ISP is two IP addresses on your single connection. This allows you to use a switch to physically split the connection, and permits each router to get its own distinct IP address. This sets up two completely separate networks, isolated from one another.

Unfortunately, being able to get multiple IP addresses on a consumer-grade internet connection is rare, and also likely to confuse your ISP salesperson.

You can accomplish the same thing without a switch (or the confusion) by purchasing two completely separate internet connections from your ISP, or two separate internet connections from two separate ISPs.

But that seems like overkill.

Split the network by using a second router

If your router doesn't support guest networks, and your ISP doesn't support multiple IP addresses, and you don't want to pay for a second separate internet connection, here is a way to jury-rig a solution using two routers.

Normally, we plug the WAN side of a router into the internet, but it doesn't have to be that way. You can plug your router into another router.

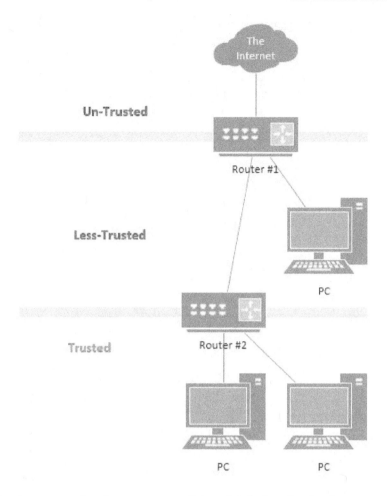

In this case, the internet feeds to router #1, which feeds the less-trusted guest or kids network. The WAN (or "internet") side of router #2 is connected to the LAN side of router #1. Trusted computers are connected to router #2.

In this diagram, connections can only be established upwards, towards the internet. All the PCs in this diagram connect to the internet. Connections cannot be established downward, meaning that everyone is protected from connections attempting to come in from the internet. More importantly, the less-trusted network cannot establish connections into the trusted. (In theory, trusted PCs devices would be able to connect to less-trusted devices, but that's generally impractical for a variety of reasons.)

Internet of things

You wouldn't expect your fridge or television set to be a security or privacy risk, but now it's quite possible. Internet-connected appliances are becoming more and more popular, and unfortunately, security seems to be only an afterthought.

The good news is that we've yet to hear about IoT devices being used to attack other devices on local networks; to date, attacks have used them to cause trouble on the public internet. However, it's easy to imagine future scenarios in which the threat may strike closer to home.

When it comes to internet-connected devices:
- Disconnect them from the internet if the functionality provided isn't being used, or isn't worth it. Most "smart TVs", for example, continue to work just fine without being connected.
- If they are going to be connected, consider treating them as the "less trusted" devices we've discussed above. Connect them to your guest network, for example.
- If you must connect them to your trusted network, make sure the other devices sharing the network are appropriately protected.

In most cases, that "appropriate protection" takes the form of a firewall.

Firewalls

The computers and devices that share a network are not protected from each other. If your computers are all safely connected to a "trusted" network, they're still vulnerable to each other. That network relies on trust, and if that trust is violated by accidentally installing malware, or doing something else risky, other computers on that network could be exposed.

That's why almost all PCs now come with a built-in firewall, enabled by default. This provides important protection of each machine from everything else.

Software firewalls, such as Windows' own firewall, are good—and, indeed, they've become progressively better with each release of Windows—but they're still not the same caliber as the natural firewall provided by a router; you need both.

Software firewalls are perfect for protecting your machines from one another, however.

PRIVACY ISSUES: ONLINE SERVICES

Privacy issues were born the moment one computer connected to another. In the decades since, with the rise of the internet and online services (often referred to with the over-hyped marketing term "the cloud"), issues have ballooned to a scale never imagined.

It's safe to say that the majority of what we do today with our computers and related devices takes place online. This exposes our information to a cast of characters, ranging from the seemingly benign to the clearly malicious, with all variants in between.

It's important to understand exactly what control we do and don't have, who we should and shouldn't trust, and perhaps what online services we should and shouldn't consider.

How Do I Protect Myself from My ISP?

> _"I know you'll think I'm nuts, but I'm absolutely convinced my ISP is snooping on what I do and reporting it to the government. I know you said my ISP can see everything, but ... how do I stop them?"_

This is a composite question crafted from the many variations on the theme that, over the years, keep coming from time to time.

While I don't actually think people are nuts, I do think that 99% of the time, they are mistaken, misled, or misinformed.

The 1%, however, can be all too real for some people.

Your ISP really doesn't care

For at least 99% of internet users: your ISP doesn't care what you do, where you go, or what you use their connection for. You and I just aren't that interesting. No one is watching you. No one is monitoring your online behavior. No one is updating your "permanent record" with your digital exploits.

If you look carefully at the terms of service you probably agreed to when you established your internet connectivity, you'll probably see there are a couple of things your ISP does care about—the most blatant being excessive use for whatever account type you have. So, in that sense, they might be keeping loose track of how many bytes you upload or download over some period of time. If you exceed some threshold, they might tap you on the shoulder and ask you to slow down, or pay more, or in the worse case, find a different ISP. Or they might just slow your connection.

But chances are they're not looking at what you're doing—just keeping an eye on how much.

Your ISP may also respond to complaints about your usage, some of which we'll see next, but it's not something they proactively look for. They have better things to do with their time and resources.

When your ISP does care

There are some things an ISP might choose to care about—either on their own, in response to complaints, or at the request of others.

- Large media companies might ask your ISP to track large downloads to identify people downloading copyrighted material.
- If they suspect you are involved in some kind of criminal activity, law enforcement agencies might ask—or even require—your ISP to track your activity.
- Overly oppressive governments might require ISPs to monitor the actions of their citizens more actively.

Of course, your employer can certainly monitor your usage of the connections they provide for a variety of reasons, as can public or private institutions like libraries, internet cafés, or others.

Perhaps more realistically, since anyone who provides your connection to the internet *is your ISP*, your landlord, the hotel's IT "department", or the stranger in the corner at a coffee shop with Wi-Fi could all just be nosy, for whatever reason.

Then what?

Option 1: Choose a different ISP

The first, knee-jerk reaction is that if you don't trust your ISP, find another ISP.

In some cases, that's simply not practical. In areas that have a monopoly provider, you might only have one choice.

Switching may also not be practical. Often, when there are alternate providers, the cost, performance, or service differential is high. You might find yourself an ISP you can trust, only to find their offerings come with significantly slower speeds or reliability.

Switching may also not be cost effective. Only you can determine the relative priority of the threat versus the potential of increased costs incurred by choosing a different provider.

In a home or business environment, the options typically boil down to cable, telephone/DSL, or wireless. You'll need to take into account the different cost/performance/service tradeoffs of each.

Of course, all this assumes you can find service from an ISP that you would trust any more than the one you currently have. If you can, and they meet your needs, this option can be the simplest in the long run.

Option 2: Use a VPN

The classic solution for protecting yourself over an untrusted connection of any sort is to use a VPN, or Virtual Private Network.

When using a VPN, your device creates an encrypted connection to that VPN's servers, and all of your internet traffic is routed through that connection. All your ISP sees is that you've connected to a remote server using an encrypted protocol; it cannot see what actually transpires over that connection.

This makes a VPN a perfect solution for travelers who regularly use otherwise untrusted connections, such as those in airports, hotels, and coffee shops.

It also means a VPN is a potential solution for any untrusted connection, even if that untrusted connection is your home internet, as provided by your ISP.

VPNs are not without issues, however.

The cost of a VPN

Using a VPN typically involves two types of costs: monetary and performance—and these two costs are often at odds.

There are free VPN services out there, but they often have poor performance. Spending money to purchase a VPN subscription typically means you'll get better service and speeds.

This ends up becoming important, because when using a VPN, you're adding an additional layer of complexity to everything being communicated over your internet connection. The data itself is "wrapped" in a layer of encryption, and it's all routed through extra servers run by the VPN. While slower speeds are perhaps tolerable periodically while traveling, if you're constantly using a VPN at home, you probably want it to impact your experience as little as possible.

The privacy of a VPN

One thing many people overlook is that when using a VPN, in a very real sense that VPN *becomes* your ISP. While the ISP can no longer see everything you do, the VPN service can. All of your internet activity is routed through their servers.

Therefore, it's important to select a VPN provider you trust—presumably more than you trust your ISP.

What your ISP can still see

There's one important thing your ISP can most definitely see that there's simply no practical way around: your ISP can see that you're using a VPN. In fact, they can probably see which VPN service you're using.

Indeed, some governments have gone so far as to outlaw VPN connections, or to block as many VPN providers as they can keep track of, to prevent you from bypassing their mandated monitoring.

Option 3: Don't use your ISP

This is the most cumbersome, and perhaps even impractical, option. In a way, it's really the same as option #1, but with more legwork.

If you can't get an alternate ISP for your location, and using a VPN isn't an appropriate approach for you, then the only real solution is to go elsewhere. By that, I mean when you want to use the internet, take a laptop to a location with an ISP you can trust.

What that might be, I can't tell you. It could be the coffee shop or library down the street—but then you'd probably want that VPN. It could be a friend's house, or your place of work—again, as long as their ISPs are more trustworthy to you.

But if you can't "fix" or bypass the internet connection at home, and you can't trust it, then you shouldn't use it... at least not for anything you consider sensitive.

Postscript: I'm soaking in it

I trust my ISP. I trust that my ISP cares little about me, as long as I pay my bills and cause them no problems. As a result, while I have a subscription to a VPN service (TunnelBear), I don't regularly use it at home.

I decided to try it out while researching and writing this chapter, so I enabled the VPN here on my desktop at home. I confirmed (via my own "what's my IP address" page) that my IP address had changed, and that I was indeed connecting to the internet from a different location—New York, it would appear, as opposed to my ISP's normal point of presence here in Washington State.

Everything kept working, albeit ever so slightly more slowly. My web browsing continued; my remote server connections disconnected when the change was made, but quickly reconnected and continued to work; Dropbox, OneDrive, and Google Drive[22] all reconnected and kept on synchronizing.

Running everything through a VPN is possible, but as I said, it's unlikely you actually need to; and which one to trust is also going to be a function of your specific situation as well.

⊙

---

[22] Yes, I use all three. And more. Sometimes being a geek can be … complicated. ☺

How Does a VPN Protect Me?

So there's a lot of talk about using a VPN to hide what we do from our ISPs, and you've mentioned using it when using open WiFi. So just how and what are the protections of this versus just connecting through my ISP? What limitations does this have? Can they "see" what I'm doing (like using a BitTorrent), and that is coming from my account?

A VPN, or Virtual Private Network, is one approach to securely connect to a remote resource. Depending on the VPN, that privacy can extend from one end of the connection to the other, or it can protect you only for a certain portion.

I'll describe the different scenarios and how you are, and perhaps are not, protected by a VPN.

No VPN at all

I'll use this scenario as the base: you're in an open WiFi hotspot, connecting to a remote resource like your email, or your bank.

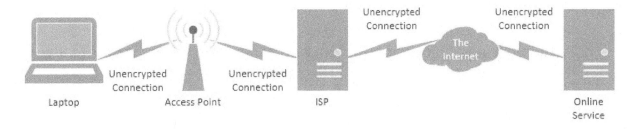

All the connections are unencrypted. That includes:
- The connection from your laptop to the wireless access point (aka hotspot).
- The connection from the wireless access point to the ISP providing the internet connection.
- The connection from that ISP to the rest of the internet.
- The connection to the specific service you're using.

The largest area of concern is the connection from your laptop to the WiFi access point. That open WiFi signal traveling through the air can be "sniffed" (or read) by anyone in range with a laptop and the appropriate software.

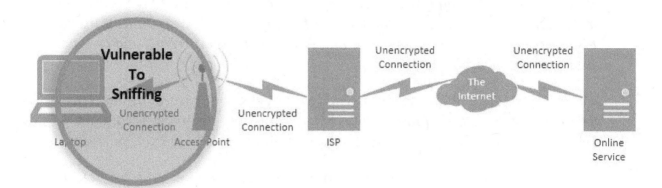

However, there's also concern about the fact that your ISP can monitor what you're doing. Specifically, they can see every remote site or service you connect to, and can examine all data not otherwise encrypted you exchange with those servers.

WPA encryption

The traditional approach to protect yourself from open WiFi sniffing is to use WPA[23] encryption built into the WiFi specification.

This secures the path between your computer and the WiFi's access point. Hopefully, it's how your home WiFi is configured, so as to prevent nearby homes or others from connecting to your WiFi, and through it, to your network, without the appropriate encryption password.

There are problems with this approach:
- Most open hotspots at coffee shops, airports, and elsewhere don't use encryption; the password requirement would confuse their customers more than it's worth. That's why these hotspots are called "open".
- When WPA is used, it protects only the connection between your computer and the WiFi access point. Everything past that point in the diagram above remains "in the clear".

---

[23] Ideally, WPA2, but that's a detail that doesn't impact our conceptual discussion.

That last point becomes important because all the traffic is visible to the hotspot's owner, should he or she care to peek, and to the internet service provider to which that hotspot is connected.

A VPN service

To protect yourself further, a VPN is a common solution.

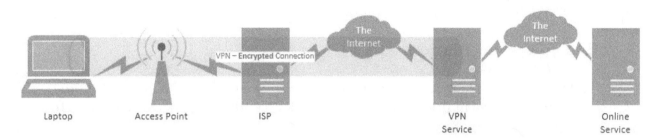

A VPN securely encrypts the entire path from your computer to the VPN provider. No one along that path can see your data: not other WiFi users, not the people managing the hotspot, and not the hotspot's ISP.

For open WiFi, or other situation with questionable security (such as connecting to the internet at your hotel), a VPN can be a great solution.

But it's not perfect.

There are some things to note:
- The connection is only secured up to the VPN's servers; the connection from the VPN provider's servers to the final destination is once again unencrypted. That means the VPN provider, as well as any other networking equipment along the rest of the way, may be able to see your data, and can at least see which servers you're connecting to.
- You're adding steps between your computer and the server you're accessing. The practical effect of this is that your connection becomes slower. How much slower varies based on the VPN service you're using, their capacity, and the server you're attempting to access.
- Not all VPN services support all protocols. For example, your web browsing might work, but your attempts to use BitTorrent might not.
- Not all remote servers allow connections through VPNs. One non-security-related reason to use a VPN is it can make you appear as if you're located

in another country. As a result, many services—such as streaming video services—block connections using VPNs.

- Not all governments allow VPN connections out of their countries, so as to effectively censor what their residents can view.

The ISP you're connecting through can't see, for example, that you're using BitTorrent, but the VPN service can. Your ISP would still see that:

- You're using a VPN (and which VPN service you're using).
- You're sending and receiving an awful lot of data.

End-to-end encryption

The only true privacy is achieved with end-to-end encryption. Unfortunately, that isn't possible in many cases, since it must be supported by the service to which you are connecting.

Http**s** is end-to-end encryption.

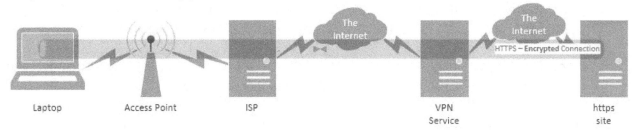

Connections you make via http**s** are completely encrypted along the entire path from your machine to the remote server you're accessing. That's why banks (and other services that allow you to access sensitive data) should use https. Most web-based email providers also provide full https connectivity. In fact, more and more sites—including *Ask Leo!*—are switching to support https.

Similarly, when configuring a POP3, IMAP, or SMTP connection in your email program, if your email provider supports it, choose SSL or TLS. That's the underlying encryption protocol used by secure connections like https. That way, your email uploads and downloads (as well as your log-in information) is completely encrypted along the entire path to your mail server.

Note, however, that even when using https, your ISP can still see which sites you connect to. Only a VPN can hide that information from them.

Https over a VPN?

Just to complete the picture, if you're using a VPN, and you happen to connect to an https web site, your data is doubly encrypted for part of the trip.

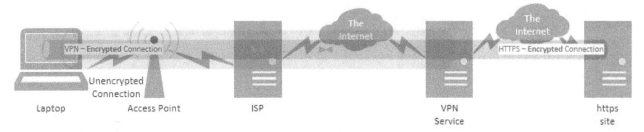

- The VPN protects you between your computer and the VPN service.
- Https protects you between your computer and the service to which you're connecting.

There's really no practical harm. One benefit is that the VPN prevents your ISP from seeing which site you're connecting to.

How Do I Encrypt Email?

"What software do you use to encrypt email? Do you have any recommendations for email encryption software (preferably free)?"

I really wish this was easier.

It should be easier.

But it's not.

The fact is, encrypting email is cumbersome, and solutions that should work easily don't work consistently. I'll look at why encrypting email matters, and then I'll give you some alternatives, starting with the one that's the easiest to use.

Why encrypt email?

An https connection to your mail account only encrypts the information between your computer and the mail server. Email itself is sent and stored in plain, unencrypted text. While on your mail provider's server, and on your recipient's server, the email is visible to mail service personnel.

On top of that, you have no control over whether any encryption is used when transmitting that mail from server to server. In theory, anyone with access to the network path taken to make the transfer could "listen in" and view your messages.

Finally, you have no control over how your recipient connects to their email. If they don't use a secure connection, they could easily be downloading your email in the clear.

If you're looking for complete security for your messages, the only solution is to encrypt the email message itself.

Unfortunately, that's not as easy as it sounds.

Encrypted attachments

By far the most practical way to encrypt email for the average user is to send your message as an encrypted attachment.

- **Write** your message in a program like Notepad, Word, or whatever text or document editor you prefer.
- **Save** that message to a file on your hard disk (example: message.txt for notepad, or message.docx for a Word document).
- Encrypt that file using a tool like 7-Zip, or even GnuPG.
- **Email** the encrypted file, as an attachment, to its destination.
- **Convey** the password or encryption key to the recipient *by some other means*. This is important: if a malicious individual captures the encrypted package, they may be able to capture the password, if you sent it using the same technique. Pick up the phone, send a letter, text, instant message, or use completely different email accounts on both ends using completely different computers in completely different locations.

There are, naturally, a couple of caveats.

Make sure you chose an encryption program your recipient can use. Your recipient will need to be able to run the corresponding decryption tool.

Make sure you choose an appropriately difficult password/passphrase. Just like account log-in passwords, encryption passwords are subject to brute-force attacks. The simpler your password, the easier it is for someone to decipher it and decrypt your message.

This process is not pretty, and the steps involved make it a barrier to doing regularly, but it works.

With that out of the way, let's look at two approaches that more closely match how it *should* work.

Certificate-based encryption

Buried in the advanced security dialogs in Outlook and account security setting dialogs in Thunderbird (and similar places in some other email clients) is the concept of using digital certificates to sign and encrypt email.

These are, essentially, the same kind of certificates used to protect https websites, and in general, they're purchased the same way. Like website certificates, these certificates can be used for two purposes:

- To digitally "sign" your messages to confirm you as the author of the message, and confirm the message has not changed since you signed it. (This isn't encryption, it's validation.)
- To allow people to send you encrypted messages such that only you can decrypt them.

That last one is a little counterintuitive. To encrypt a message, you don't use your own encryption certificate; you use that of the person to whom you're sending the encrypted message. That way, only they can decrypt it. (In reality, certificate-based encryption, like https, is quite complex and relies on public key cryptography, discussed below.)

This is a fine approach, and once set up, can be nearly transparent. As long as both you and your recipient use the same encryption mechanism, your emails are transparently encrypted and decrypted when sent or viewed. While stored on your machine, on your recipient's machine, or somewhere in between, the messages are securely encrypted.

Unfortunately, it suffers from a couple of problems preventing widespread adoption:

- Not all email programs and interfaces support it.
- Certificates either cost money, or are cumbersome to obtain.
- All parties involved need to use the same system for it to work.

PGP/GPG-based encryption

PGP (Pretty Good Privacy) and GPG (Gnu Privacy Guard, the open-source equivalent) are very similar to the certificate-based encryption scheme above. They rely on public key cryptography, which, in a nutshell, boils down to this:

Two really large numbers, A and B, are created, and share a special relationship:
- Anything encrypted with "A" can only be decrypted by "B".
- Anything encrypted with "B" can only be decrypted by "A".

You make either A or B public, and keep the other one private.

Let's say I make my "A" number public ([which I have]), and keep the "B" number private—only I have it. You can now encrypt a message to me using my public key "A". Only I can decrypt it with my private key "B".

To encrypt email to someone, you need their public key (their "A", in my example). For someone to send an email only you can decrypt, they need your public key. The private key ("B") is needed to decrypt it.

PGP and GPG are just standard techniques and tools to manage those two "numbers", more commonly called keys, or key pairs.

The good news about GPG is that all the parts are free. The bad news it can be ~~fairly~~ really geeky. I wrote an article about using it some years ago: [How do I send encrypted email?], which walks through the steps. I don't recommend it for the average user, but if you're at all technical, or just enjoy this kind of geekery, you can see what it entails.

Most email programs do not include support for GPG/PGP keys. Thunderbird does have an extension, "[Enigmail]", that adds support quite nicely, and there's a Chrome browser extension called "Mailvelope" that adds encryption to Gmail.

The weakest link when you encrypt email

I have to include a word about *trust*.

All the encryption in the world won't help a whit if you can't trust the person at the receiving end. They have to keep passwords safe, if you use them, and they have to keep your private message private, if that's the intent of your encryption. They also have to practice safe computing—your message will be decrypted on their computer, and hence visible to any malware that might be present there. Heck, if their computer is stolen and they happened to keep the decrypted message, that email is now in the hands of someone else.

So, in addition to doing the right things with your sensitive information *yourself*, make sure your recipient has an appropriate level of understanding as well.

That's something technology just can't fix.

Securing Your Data in the Cloud

One of the hidden issues in online storage is privacy. Specifically, almost all online storage providers have the ability to examine your data or hand it over to law enforcement, *even if the provider has encrypted your data.*

Hopefully, most of us will never have to deal with the law-enforcement scenario, but even the realization that a rogue employee at an online data storage provider could peek into what we keep online can cause concern. For some, it's enough concern to avoid using cloud storage at all.

The solution is simple: encrypt the data yourself.

Unfortunately, implementing that "simple" solution isn't always that simple or transparent, and can add a layer of complexity to online storage some find just as intimidating.

BoxCryptor is a nicely unobtrusive encryption solution, and free for personal use.

The hidden issue

Online[24] storage is powerful when used properly. By "properly," I mean the account used is set up with appropriate security, and the data you place online is backed up somewhere else as well. Ignoring either of those items can lead to permanent data loss, or worse.

Even with those basics covered, though, a potential privacy issue remains. Unless you take additional steps of your own, the provider of that online service has the ability to view your data.

- Your data may not be encrypted, and is stored in view of anyone with administrative access to the service provider's servers.
- Your data may be encrypted by the service provider, but *since it's encrypted by the service provider*, it can also be *decrypted* by the service provider. As a result, those with administrative access still have the ability to view your data.

---

[24] The over-hyped marketing term "cloud" is really nothing more than a replacement for "online". What is often called "cloud storage" is really nothing more than storage provided by online services.

In reality, the folks at major online storage providers are professionals, with no interest in snooping around in your data. Instances of the so-called "rogue employee" are rare. But of course, it's still possible.

More legitimately, the service provider may be *required* to turn over your unencrypted data to law enforcement should the appropriate court orders be presented.[25]

For whatever reason, you might consider all of this a problem. Fortunately, this problem has a solution: encryption.

The hidden cost of doing your own encryption

There's one good reason to allow your online storage provider to decrypt your data: web access.

If your online storage provider encrypts your data when it's stored on their servers, they must be able to decrypt it to provide you the ability to access the data via a web interface. Dropbox, for example, allows you to log in to your account from any machine and access the files stored in your account via the web.

If you encrypt the data yourself using BoxCryptor, the online storage provider can only access your data in its encrypted form. You'll need BoxCryptor on your computer (and of course, your password) to decrypt it before you'll be able to use that data.

Traditional encryption solutions

The idea here is simply that if **you** encrypt your data before it gets uploaded to any online storage provider, they have no ability to decrypt it. You, and only you[26], control the access to your actual data.

Traditionally, that works this way:
- You have a file or set of files that you want to store online.

---

[25] Depending on the laws in your locality, of course.
[26] And of course, anyone with whom you choose to share the password.

- You use a program such as 7-zip, TrueCrypt, or similar to create a new file or files containing encrypted versions of the files.
- You place those files into online storage.

Now, when you want to actually use those files on any machine where you don't have the original, or want to make sure you have the most current copy, you need to:
- Retrieve the encrypted files from online storage.
- Decrypt the files.
- Make your changes.

Then, finally, to update the online copies of the files (if you made any changes), you would:
- Re-encrypt the files as you did originally.
- Upload the encrypted file or files into online storage.

As you can see, that's a lot of work just to update, for example, a single file.

That's where BoxCryptor comes in.

> **Isn't TrueCrypt Dead?**
>
> Yes. Yes it is. I now recommend using VeraCrypt in place of TrueCrypt. I use "TrueCrypt" as a description for the general technique used by both TrueCrypt, and its successors, including VeraCrypt.

The BoxCryptor model

In a sense, BoxCryptor operates in a manner very similar to TrueCrypt.

To use TrueCrypt, you create a special container and tell TrueCrypt to mount that container as a virtual drive, supplying the correct passphrase to do so. A new drive appears on your system—say drive T:—and the contents of the encrypted container appear as unencrypted files. As long as the container is mounted, the contents of the "vault" are directly accessible to any and all programs running on your machine. Dismount or fail to mount the container, and all that's visible is the vault file itself, which appears to contain only random noise.

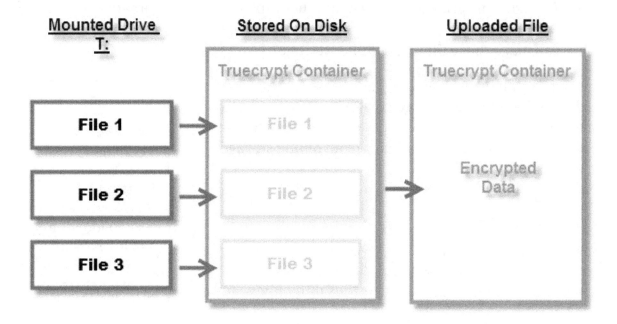

BoxCryptor works similarly, except that the container is nothing more than a source folder: any other folder on your machine. You mount that folder in BoxCryptor and another drive—I'll call it L:—appears on your machine. Anything written to drive L: is encrypted and written to the folder you specified when mounting. Anything read from that drive causes the corresponding encrypted file in the source folder to be read and decrypted on the fly.

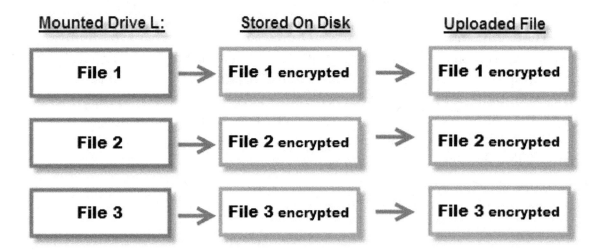

While technically slightly inaccurate, you can think of BoxCryptor as operating like TrueCrypt, but at the encrypted file, rather than encrypted container, level.

The files in the original source folder are always encrypted. It's only when the folder is mounted in BoxCryptor that the files are visible in their decrypted form in the virtual drive.

An example of BoxCryptor in use

Let's say I use Dropbox. On my machine, I have a folder:

>   C:\My Dropbox

In that folder, I have many other files and folders that are automatically synchronized with the Dropbox servers and any other machines on which I have Dropbox installed.

One of the folders in my Dropbox folder is:

>   C:\My Dropbox\Boxcryptor Files

I don't place any files in the Boxcryptor Files folder directly. It starts out empty.

Next, I install BoxCryptor, and configure it to mount "C:\My Dropbox\Boxcryptor Files" as drive L:. I set up the password required to mount it again in the future.

Drive L: appears on my machine.

I then create a Word document on drive L:

>   L:\MyPrivateInformation.docx

As soon as I save that document to drive L: using Word, a new file appears on C::

>   C:\My Dropbox\Boxcryptor Files\MyPrivateInformation.docx

The file that was saved to L: is automatically encrypted and placed in the BoxCryptor folder. Dropbox notices a new file has appeared, and the *encrypted* file is then also uploaded and distributed to all my machines running Dropbox. Note that only the *encrypted* version of the file has been uploaded.

I can continue to work on the file on L: to my heart's content. In a very real sense, it's just a file, and can be manipulated like any other. As changes are saved to disk, the corresponding encrypted version of the file is updated appropriately.

Once I *dis*mount the BoxCryptor folder, drive L:—along with the unencrypted versions of the files—disappears. All that remains are the encrypted versions stored in the BoxCryptor folder within the Dropbox folder.

All that has been uploaded to your online storage provider are the encrypted versions of your files.

TrueCrypt or BoxCryptor?

There's a reasonable argument that you can use BoxCryptor for almost anything that you might use a standard TrueCrypt vault for.

The practical differences boil down to this:
- **Monolithic versus incremental update**: the biggest drawback to using TrueCrypt with a service such as Dropbox is that it's a single file. Any changes to *any* of the files contained within it means that the entire file may be considered changed and may need to be uploaded or downloaded. BoxCryptor maintains individual files as individual files; thus, only files that are actually modified need updating.
- **Open- versus closed-source**: TrueCrypt is an open-source project, and its source code can be examined and audited. BoxCryptor is a commercial product from a German company, so using BoxCryptor requires you implicitly trust this company.

It's also my understanding that TrueCrypt, besides having more encryption options, has more highly-tuned performance.

TrueCrypt is free no matter what you do with it. While BoxCryptor's base version is free, there are licensing levels for additional features, as well as for commercial use.

In short, BoxCryptor is an excellent solution for encrypting files that are going to be placed in online storage management utilities such as DropBox. In my opinion, TrueCrypt remains the better choice for encrypting offline data. And of course, it's entirely possible to use both side by side.

It's for more than PCs

Like many online services similar to Dropbox, BoxCryptor supports multiple platforms.

BoxCryptor is available for:
- Windows
- Apple OSX
- Android
- iPad and iPhone

That means you can continue to share your documents across all the platforms and devices supported by your online storage provider, but now you can easily encrypt the data you share.

It's free for personal use, but...

I actually recommend you spring for the personal license.

Besides better support, it includes a feature I suspect many people might want: filename encryption.

As you saw above, my example document:

> L:\MyPrivateInformation.docx

was saved as:

> C:\My Dropbox\Boxcryptor Files\MyPrivateInformation.docx

In other words, the name of the file remains visible.

For many, that might not be a problem, but for others, names of files (and folders) represent an unexpected way sensitive information can leak out, even if the contents of those documents are encrypted.

When you purchase the "Unlimited Personal" license, file names are instead stored encrypted. For example, my example document might appear as:

> C:\My Dropbox\Boxcryptor Files\gVbJ27u6-VMQ

Only when successfully mounted will the file names once again appear unencrypted (on drive L:, to continue the examples above).

And of course, there's a commercial license as well.

How I use BoxCryptor

I've been using BoxCryptor for a couple of years.

Much like in the example above, I have a folder in my cloud synchronization[27] folder dedicated to the files I wish BoxCryptor to store encrypted.

I have BoxCryptor installed on my Windows PCs as well as my Macs.

Using BoxCryptor allows me to feel secure leveraging online storage and using it for even more things—things I wouldn't necessarily place into a large monolithic TrueCrypt container, but would still hesitate to upload unencrypted.

BoxCryptor is a convenient solution for making sure the data you place in online storage services remains secure and is accessible only by you.

I recommend it.

⊙

---

[27] While I still use Dropbox for a lot, I actually use "SyncThing" for my more secure information, as it allows me to use my own server as online storage.

Is It Time to Start Using an Adblocker?

One of the positions I've held for as long as *Ask Leo!* been around is that adblockers are fundamentally wrong. They prevent sites that depend on advertising from making the revenue they need to survive.

Let's be clear about one thing up front: this isn't about greed. This is about survival.

Many useful websites exist solely because of the advertising revenue they're able generate. If that goes away, the sites go away. Rarely does advertising on small- and medium-sized sites cover more than the basic costs.

If you consider viewing advertisements as the "cost" of consuming the content you want for free, then blocking those ads can rightfully be considered theft. You're using the content without paying the price.

That's been my position for years.

But, at the risk of being hypocritical, I'm starting to change my mind. And the advertisers have no one to blame but themselves.

Success is their downfall

My position to date has been that if you don't like the advertisements on a site, then don't visit that site. "Vote with your feet." Go to another site that has less annoying ads, or pay for a site that has as an option to remove ads[28].

There are sites with useful information that I don't visit, reference, or point people to, simply because the advertising on those sites is so bad.

However, voting with your feet doesn't solve the underlying problem. Because ads are so ubiquitous, so many web sites use the same ad networks, and so many ad networks use the same techniques, it's become nearly impossible to find alternative sites that actually meet the criteria of less-annoying ads.

---

[28] I don't currently offer that option, primarily because it means every paying visitor would need an account (another account for you to manage), and the impact on the server of managing each account's access would require me to pay more for a more powerful server. Besides, as you'll see, I have a compromise.

You can run, but you can't hide.

Manipulation is their downfall

For many years, one of the techniques used by advertisers in the tech space was to make their ads look like download buttons. Visit a site to get the latest download of your favorite image-burning software, and you'll see half a dozen nearly indistinguishable DOWNLOAD buttons, only one of which is the "real" download button you want. The rest? Ads.

My sense is that this has improved somewhat, but the problem remains: ads don't always look like ads. They try to manipulate visitors into thinking the ad is part of the content. This is why it's important to learn to recognize ads.

Manipulation also appears in another guise called "sponsored content". This is content someone pays to place on a web site.[29] Sometimes it's obvious, but often it's indistinguishable from the site's own content. What you think is a legitimate recommendation or evaluation of a product may really be an article written by that product's creator. In other words, it might be an ad.

Tracking is their downfall

As long-time readers know, I'm not terribly concerned about the tracking that results in ads "following me" around the internet. But I know they concern some. To many, it feels like an invasion of privacy, and to others, it just feels creepy.

The problem, of course, is that the technique works. Ads that follow people are effective. And because they're effective, more and more advertisers and advertising networks use the technique to sell more of whatever it is they're selling. As more and more advertisers use it, more and more ads start "following" you. Even though it really is benign, the result is that the internet feels creepier and creepier.

---

[29] Something I've never accepted on *Ask Leo!,* and have no plans of accepting in the future. All Ask Leo! content currently originates exclusively from me. If that ever changes, it'll be obvious.

As an advertising-supported site, it also means I have even less control over what ads appear here. The ads that "follow" you might have nothing to do with technology, or anything I've ever even heard of. You may see ads here for all manner of things, for good or bad.

Malware is their downfall

Honestly, the final straw breaking my adblocking back is malware. It doesn't happen often, but we've definitely heard of situations where an ad isn't an ad at all, but rather a conduit for installing malware on your machine.

This can happen for either of two reasons:
- An advertising network, or the software it uses to display ads on your machine, gets hacked into displaying malicious ads.
- An advertising network has insufficient safeguards in place, and advertisers are unintentionally allowed to display ads that are malicious.

The reason this concerns me is not because it's common—it's not—but that it's almost completely out of your control.

I've long taught that you can't get into trouble if you only visit reputable sites. But if that site happens to use an ad network that's somehow compromised, that's no longer. And there's no way to know beforehand.

My *Ask Leo!* compromise

As a website owner, I know adblockers are inevitable, and in the face of malware, they're more and more difficult to argue against.

If you visit *Ask Leo!* with an adblocker turned on, in place of the ads I normally use to pay for the site from Google's Adsense program[30], you'll see a static image asking you to consider becoming a patron to help support the site.

I know other sites—particularly news sites—get more aggressive, often showing a pop-up to visitors using an adblocker. I've seen a handful go so far as to actually block access completely if you're using an adblocker.

---

[30] Ironically, as I write this, I'm also testing a program from Adsense that occasionally places a little "Can you help us?" tab at the bottom of the screen as an additional way to solicit support. It's ironic because many adblockers block this as well.

How do I know this?

Because for the last few months I've been test-driving an adblocker.

What adblocker to use?

I really, really, wanted to be able to use Privacy Badger from the Electronic Frontier Foundation. As its name implies, it's focused not on ad blocking, but on maintaining your privacy. Its approach is heuristic, meaning it looks for website behavior that looks like tracking and blocks it. As it turns out, there's a high degree of overlap between advertising and tracking techniques, so it functions as a relatively effective ad blocker as well.

Sadly, it's pretty close to an everything-blocker or everything-breaker. The problem is that Privacy Badger is quite aggressive, and many techniques used to detect tracking are valid for other purposes as well. For example, a technique I use here on *Ask Leo!*—to speed up the site by using a content delivery network— is detected as tracking by Privacy Badger. As a result, visiting *Ask Leo!* would result in a jumbled mess on your screen.

Yes, you can whitelist things, but so many sites break, and it's such a frustrating exercise to try and figure out what to whitelist (would you know to whitelist med.askleomedia.com and img.askleomedia.com to get *Ask Leo!* to work?), Privacy Badger is simply a non-starter for the average computer user.

Give it a try if you like, but expect lots of things to break.

What I've settled on is uBlock Origin (not to be confused with uBlock). Technically, it's not "just" an adblocker; in their words, it's "… a wide-spectrum blocker … default behavior of uBlock Origin when newly installed is to block ads, trackers and malware sites". It's a browser add-on that runs quietly in the background as web pages are displayed. It's lightweight, has a good reputation, and doesn't break too much.

Unfortunately, it does break some things. But the mechanism to whitelist, or temporarily whitelist, a site in order to make it work is simple and effective. (Click the uBlock Origin icon in the browser, and then click an "off" icon.) And it's quite configurable.

More to the point, after running it for a couple of months (in Google Chrome, but there are versions for FireFox as well) my browsing experience was not seriously impacted, except for the occasional "we see you're using an adblocker" message. Rarely did I need to whitelist a site I was visiting, and that was easy and quick.

Where do we go from here?

Internet advertising is broken.

Between sites plastered with ads, the perception of privacy issues, misleading and manipulative advertisements, and the risk—however small—of malware, it's hard to say anything else.

Advertising has also enabled the varied and rich experience that is the internet today. Without ads, a significant number of the sites you rely on daily—perhaps even most of them—simply wouldn't exist.

As a website owner, I have to be pragmatic to keep my site and service afloat. Ads allowed *Ask Leo!* to come into being, and ads in some form will certainly be here as long as I can envision. At the same time, I'm not taking any draconian actions against those who choose to use adblockers—I get it, I really do. In my case, I simply explore other ways to pay the bills, be it books, services, or direct patronage.

As an internet user, I've become much less averse to financially supporting the sites and services I use that give me value. Be it subscriptions, purchases, or patronage, I believe it's important to put my money where my mouth is. If advertising is broken—and it is—then these same sites and services are almost certainly dealing with the same kinds of issues I am.

I know how the sausage is made, and it takes money to turn the crank.

PRIVACY ISSUES: THE OTHER END OF THE CONNECTION

The Biggest Risk to Your Privacy

From the computers we use to the systems that run them, as well as the applications and tools we rely on, each adds risk of some kind of exposure.

And yet, in my experience, the greatest risk we're exposed to has little do with technology.

It's a risk we don't think of—and yet I see privacy directly invaded more often due to this than any other reason.

The biggest risk is people

Even with semi-regular news of data breaches, hacking, and other technological intrusions, the single biggest cause for actual tangible privacy-related damage boils down to nothing more than... people.

I'm certain you're already making assumptions about which people you should be concerned about. I'm just as certain you're overlooking perhaps the most important group that puts our privacy at risk every day.

Let's review some of the various classes of people involved in putting our privacy at risk.

Hackers, scammers, and other ne'er-do-wells

This is the first thing people think of when it comes to privacy invasions. We hear a seemingly endless stream of news and word-of-mouth reports of privacy hacks every day. It's easy to think we're under constant threat from evil villains trying to get at our data.

In a sense, we are. There's no question that organized crime and other malicious entities have their sights set on gathering personal information and using that for nefarious purposes directly, or reselling it to those who would.

While your data could fall victim to the individuals in this category, it's important to realize they're simply not interested in *you* as an individual. What they're interested in is much broader; what they care about is gathering as much data as they can, or scamming as many people as they can. Particularly when it comes to scams, *they don't care who those people are—* just that they're vulnerable.

Perhaps in part due to the obviousness of this class, this is the group of people we most easily protect ourselves from, using technology and common sense. Security software of various flavors and layers, coupled with skepticism and our own smart habits, are our first, best line of defense.

Governments and government agencies

You may think I'm including this because I'm concerned your government is spying on you.

I'm not.

Oh, it's certainly possible, and in some countries even plausible, depending on your own behavior and "value" to whomever might be watching. Once again, however, I believe strongly that most of us, in most countries, simply aren't that interesting (or worth the effort) for individual government surveillance. It's just not that big of an individual risk.

No, what makes government in general one of the largest threats to our privacy are the laws and policies they enact or *fail to enact*. Weak government policy and enforcement around individual rights and privacy makes it easier for others—in the government *and elsewhere*—to access and possibly misuse our personal information.

Most people never pay attention to this unless they're already living under an oppressive regime, in which case it could be considered too late. I strongly suggest that *paying attention and working within your system to ensure personal privacy rights* is an important responsibility.

Employees, technicians, and policy makers

Many people are concerned about big business and corporations collecting and using our personal information.

I'm generally not. Excepting the previous point about making sure that government regulations are in place to protect my information, and corporate policies that similarly ensure my privacy—whether a legal requirement or not—I'm actually not that concerned about the information I'm certain is out there about me.

With one exception: when those companies get hacked or otherwise compromised.

That generally comes back to the people involved. I believe the majority of breeches boil down to individual people making individual errors.

One example might be the software engineer with little to no security experience placed in charge of the security of my data. All the good intentions in the world won't make up for the inevitable oversight (which is probably more common than we suspect). Software developers and policy makers operate under a "features first, security later" approach that often pushes service development—and with it our personal information—beyond acceptable risk. Then, once a vulnerability is discovered, the hackers mentioned earlier swoop in to take advantage of the unintentional access to our information.

The most important thing you can do to secure yourself against these types of oversights is to know who you're dealing with, and hold them responsible and accountable for the security of your information. Do business with companies that have a proven track record. If you find you can't—if you find you need the services of an unproven entity—be particularly wary of the information you choose to share.

Friends and family, business contacts, and associates

We share a fair amount of information without thinking about the ramifications of exposing ourselves to other people.

Sometimes that can even be literal. I frequently encounter individuals who come to me concerned that their video chats might be intercepted by some middleman.

As it turns out, it's not the middleman they need be concerned about when they find themselves being blackmailed by the *individual at the other end of the conversation.*

The fact is, there's no technology—none whatsoever—that can protect you from the people to whom you choose to expose your information (or anything else). Any technology can be circumvented in one form or another by the recipient. *If it can be seen, it can be copied,* even if it's just taking a picture of the computer screen while your sensitive details are displayed.

And of course, once something is posted publicly (and let's be clear: all social media is "public", regardless of your privacy settings), it cannot be recalled.

This is, perhaps, the single most common cause of privacy violations I've encountered over the many years I've been doing Ask Leo!—not big business or government, not massive data breaches, not malware, not even ransomware[31]— but one-to-one interactions in which individuals share too much and later regret it.

This risk is only growing on social media, which creates an illusion of intimacy and safety while nothing of the sort exists.

You

You are the biggest risk to your own privacy.

By sharing too much on social media, or trusting too easily when some stranger calls to tell you your computer has a problem, or by reaching out to the wrong people in times of technological crisis because you're panicking, the biggest risk of all comes back to you.

And that's great!

Now, why, after what might seem like gloom and doom about all the ways our privacy can be compromised, am I so excited to point the finger at you?

Because the one thing you have control over is yourself.

---

[31] Which is just malware. Particularly destructive, but malware nonetheless.

You can become more knowledgeable. *You* can make better decisions. *You* can take responsibility for your privacy from here on out.

There's no requirement that you become a Luddite and walk away from technology in general—Lord knows I've certainly not done that. What's required is simply awareness—mindfulness, if you will—of exactly what, where, and with whom you share.

That last one is perhaps the most important: your privacy is all about the people you trust and share with.

APPENDICES

Appendix I: Source Material

Much of the information in this book was compiled from articles originally published on *Ask Leo!,* and then updated and edited for this format. For your reference, these are the articles that served as the foundation of this book. (Use search on the site to locate their specific pages.)

Join the conversation! Most of these original articles include reader comments, and I'd love to hear from you as well.

Introduction

Privacy? What Privacy? - It may seem like privacy is a thing of the past. I believe we misunderstand privacy, and can control more than we think.

Giving Away Our Privacy - We rail against intrusions into our private affairs and private information; and then post our private information publicly. Where's the logic in that?

Vulnerable Points on the Path to Privacy - Privacy and security: tracing the path from your fingertips through the services you use to your information's final destination.

What Does It Mean for a Source to be "Reputable"? - We often advise only trusting "reputable" sites, but how do you tell if a site or service has a good reputation?

Computer Software

Privacy Begins with the Operating System - Privacy is a complex and far-reaching topic. One of the most basic and often overlooked players: the operating system on your device.

Are There Hidden Files that Save Every Keystroke I've Ever Typed? - There's a lot of misinformation, and even paranoia, relating to keystroke logging and privacy. Much of it, however, is based on small kernels of truth.

<u>Adjusting Windows 10 Privacy Settings</u> - We'll look at how to review and adjust privacy settings in several areas of Win10.

<u>Every Application Adds Risk</u> - Everything you download adds risk. Use my three guidelines to be safer.

Computer Hardware

<u>Sometimes the Threat Is in the Hardware</u> - We spend a lot of time on software-related issues, but malicious activities and privacy violations can happen via hardware as well.

<u>How Do I Prevent My Internet-connected Devices from Being Hijacked?</u> - Recent attacks on the internet demonstrate that the so-called "internet of things" lacks basic security considerations.

<u>Walking Away From Your Computer</u> - If your device is not physically secure, neither are the machine or your data.

<u>7 Steps to a Secure Router</u> - Your router is your first line of defense against malicious attacks from the internet. But do you have a secure router? I'll review the important settings.

<u>How Do I Use an Open Wi-Fi Hotspot Safely?</u> - Open Wi-Fi hotspots at coffee shops, airports, and other public places are opportunities for hackers to steal information and more. I'll review how to stay safe.

Online Services

<u>How Do I Protect Myself from My ISP?</u> - If you're using an internet connection from a source you don't trust, there are a few alternatives.

<u>How Do I Encrypt Email?</u> - It's surprisingly difficult to encrypt email. We'll look at a practical solution anyone can use, as well as the way things "should" work.

<u>BoxCryptor—Secure Your Data in the Cloud</u> - Many online cloud storage providers encrypt your data, but if needed, they can decrypt it

themselves. BoxCryptor is a great solution to ensure that your online data remains private, regardless of how it's stored.

How Does a VPN Protect Me? A VPN, or Virtual Private Network, is a fully encrypted and private internet connection via a VPN provider. I'll look at what protection it offers.

Is It Time to Start Using an Adblocker? I'm changing my tune about adblockers. Internet advertising is broken.

How Do I Protect Myself from Other Computers on My Local Network? Many households have computers used for sensitive things sharing a network with less trustworthy users. Here's one method for in-home protection.

Other Privacy Issues

The Biggest Risk to Your Privacy - The biggest risk to your privacy is probably not what you think it is.

ENDNOTES

Afterword

I hope this book gives you more control over your privacy. It's close to impossible not to have some of your information exposed in some way—at least not and still use the internet—but hopefully now you'll have some tools to reduce your exposure and make knowledgeable decisions related to your privacy online.

If it's helped you at all—especially if you now feel a little more confident online—I consider this a success.

If you have found this book valuable, I'd really appreciate it if you posted a review on Amazon (http://go.askleo.com/aprivacybook). You'll be helping more people get enough knowledge to make informed decisions about their privacy.

If you find what you believe to be an error in this book, please register it (the details are in the next section) and then visit the errata page for this book. That page will list all known errors and corrections, and give you a place to report anything you've found that isn't already listed.

Register Your Book!

Having purchased this book, you're entitled to additional updates, errata, and other bonus materials:

- Updates for life.
- Regardless of how you purchased this book, you can download it in any or all of three digital formats:
  - PDF (for your computer or any device that can view PDF files)
  - .mobi (ideal for the Amazon Kindle), or
  - .epub (for a variety of other electronic reading devices).
- Other bonuses and supplementary material I might make available in the future.

Registering gives you access to it all.

Visit **https://go.askleo.com/regprivacy** *right now* and register.

That link is mentioned *only here,* and it's totally FREE to owners of this book.

About the Author

I've been writing software in various forms since 1976. In over 18 years at Microsoft, I held both managerial and programming roles in several groups, ranging from programming languages to Windows Help, Microsoft Money, and Expedia. Since 2003, I've been answering tech questions at the extremely popular *Ask Leo!* website (https://askleo.com) and in entrepreneurial projects like this book.

Curious for more? Someone asked, and I answered on the site: Who is Leo? (https://askleo.com/who-is-leo/).

Feedback, Questions, and Contacting Leo

I'd love to hear from you.

Honest.

I truly appreciate reader input, comments, feedback, corrections, and opinions— even when the opinions differ from my own!

Here's how best to contact me:

- If you have a comment or a question about this book, I strongly encourage you to register your book, as outlined in above, and use the prioritized comment form in the registered owner's center.

- If you prefer not to register your book, you can email me at leo@askleo.com.

- If you have a computer or tech-related question, the best approach by far is to first search Ask Leo! (https://askleo.com). Many, many questions are already answered right there, and finding those answers is much faster than waiting for me.

- If you can't find your answer using Search, visit https://askleo.com/book and submit your question. That's a special form just for book purchasers and it gets prioritized attention.

- If you just want to drop me a line, or have something you want to share that isn't covered above, you can use https://askleo.com/book, or email leo@askleo.com.

- If you're just not sure what to do ... email leo@askleo.com. ☺

Copyright & Administrivia

Sharing this Document

The bottom line is that you shouldn't.

More specifically, you shouldn't make copies and give them to others.

Loan your copy as you see fit. (Back it up, of course!) However, making an additional copy to *give* to someone else is a no-no. (The rule is simple: if you *loan* the book, they have access to it, and you don't, until they return it. If both you and your friend can use the book at the same time, then you've made a *copy,* and that's the part that's wrong.) That goes for uploading a copy to an electronic bulletin board, website, file sharing or similar type of service.

The information in this document is copyrighted. That means that giving copies to others is illegal. But more important than that, it's simply wrong.

Instead, if you think it's valuable enough to share, encourage your friends who need this book to buy a copy of their own. Or, heck, buy one as a gift for them.

Remember, it's the sale of valuable information in books like this one that makes Ask Leo! possible. It's simple, really; if enough people disregard that, there'd be no more books, and eventually no more Ask Leo!

More *Ask Leo!* Books

If you found this book helpful, check out my growing library of books at https://store.askleo.com.

Use the coupon code BOOKOWNER when you purchase the PDF download version from The *Ask Leo!* Store at check-out, and get *20% off* the regular price.

The list is always growing, but here are a few of my most popular titles.

⊙

The *Ask Leo!* Guide to Staying Safe on the Internet - Expanded Edition

Now in its thoroughly revised and greatly Expanded 4th Edition.

You *can* use the internet safely!

In this book, I cover the things you must do, the software you must run, and the concepts you need to be aware of to keep your computer, your data, and yourself safe as you use the internet.

It's really not that hard, and once things are in place, it's not even that time-consuming.

But it is necessary.

Five major areas are covered to keep you safe:

- Never lose precious files, emails, or data again: **Protect your data**.

- Reduce the chances of malware impacting you dramatically, and recover quickly and easily if it does: **Protect your computer**.
- Travel worry-free with your laptop and its data protected, as well as securing your internet access wherever you may be: **Protect your laptop**.
- Prevent account hacks and recover quickly when they happen through no fault of your own: **Protect your online world**.
- Learn what we mean by common sense, and never fall for scams and scammers again: **Protect yourself**.

Yes, you can use the internet with confidence and peace of mind.

The Ask Leo! Guide to Staying Safe on the Internet - Expanded Edition

Visit https://store.askleo.com for more information.

⊙

The *Ask Leo!* Tip of the Day

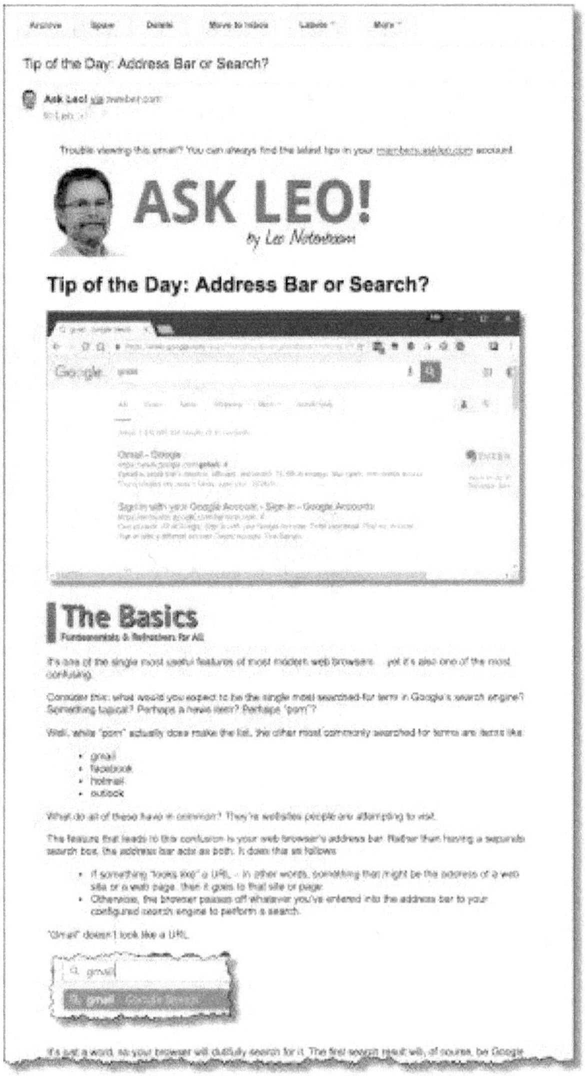

Get a tip emailed six days a week (*) to help you use your computer and your technology more effectively and with more confidence. Includes online access to *all previous tips*! (And much more … see below.)

(*) OK, OK, sometimes it might be 7 days.

The Ask Leo! Tip of the Day is designed to be a short, easy-to-digest, and above all, *useful* bit of information about using your computer, technology, or the internet more effectively and safely.

There's something for everyone, from the *beginner* to the *experienced* computer user.

In fact, one day a week, tips focus specifically on "The Basics", those tips and tricks we all take for granted, that everyone assumes; the things that, once you learn, make a dramatic impact in your understanding and use of the powerful tools in front of you.

> *Thank you, Leo, for your tips. I'm an avid follower.*
> *– Joan*

At the other end of the spectrum, once a week the tips focus on the Windows Command Prompt. From its roots in MS-DOS, Command Prompt is a powerful yet poorly understood environment. Both advanced and intermediate users will learn techniques that—to be honest —are *easier* when performed using the Command Prompt.

> *I love this tip—did not know it existed so a BIG thank you!!*
> *-Vivian*

In other tips, cover the gamut from keystrokes to security, from problem diagnosis to improving efficiency.

> *This is a cool one!*
> *-Anonymous*

And it's not just about Windows 10!

While the changes in Windows 10 certainly present many, *many*, (too many?), learning opportunities, many of the tips span Windows versions all the way back to Windows XP.

Become a patron, get tips

The *Ask Leo!* Tip of the Day is a reward offered at the Bronze level of *Ask Leo!* patronage.

> Tip of the Day*: BRILLIANT idea! Well done.*
> *-Peter*

The Bronze level of patronage includes more than just the tips:

- An email subscription to The *Ask Leo!* Tip of the Day
- Online access to the entire library of previously published tips (and reader comments, often including even more tips!)
- Any *Ask Leo!* book in digital format from the *Ask Leo!* Store, once a quarter
- Access to my other patrons-only and patron-first posts
- "Adblocker absolution"—use that ad blocker guilt free!
- Prioritized questions—yours move to the head of the line

Did you catch the one about books? That's up to four books a year—an $80 in value all by itself.

> *This is deeeelightful.*
> *-Roberta*

Plus the tips. Plus the archive. Plus priority. Plus a clear conscience.

Sign up today! Become an *Ask Leo!* patron pledging at least $5 a month, and start getting The *Ask Leo!* Tip of the Day—and everything else listed above—today.

Visit https://patreon.com/askleo.